TECHNOLOGY, MARKET STRUCTURE AND INTERNATIONALIZATION

The technological capacity of nations is increasingly seen as a crucial influence on their international competitiveness and growth prospects. Yet, technology does not receive due attention in development policy in many developing countries.

This volume discusses the domestic and external factors that impinge upon the process of technological capability building in developing countries and draws policy implications. Specifically, it examines the interaction between technological effort in developing countries and factors such as:

- trends of globalization, emergence of new technologies and stronger patent regimes;
- market structure, firm size and performance;
- affiliation with multinational enterprises and technology imports;
- international trade.

Crucially, the authors redress the balance in the current literature by providing a developing country perspective on the economic analysis of technology and considerations affecting policies.

Providing fresh insights, this volume will be of interest to researchers in development economics as well as to those involved in the formulation of policy in developing countries.

Nagesh Kumar is currently on the faculty of the United Nations University Institute for New Technologies, Maastricht, the Netherlands.
N.S. Siddharthan is Professor of Economics and Head, V.K.R.V. Rao Centre for Studies in Globalization, Institute of Economic Growth, Delhi, India.

UNU/INTECH STUDIES IN NEW TECHNOLOGY AND DEVELOPMENT
Series editors: Charles Cooper and Swasti Mitter

The books in this series reflect the research initiatives at the United Nations University Institute for New Technologies (UNU/INTECH) based in Maastricht, the Netherlands. The institute is primarily a research centre within the UN system and evaluates the social, political and economic environment in which new technologies are adopted and adapted in the developing world. The books in the series explore the role that technology policies can play in bridging the economic gap between nations, as well as between groups within nations. The authors and contributors are leading scholars in the field of technology and development; their work focuses on:

- the social and economic implications of new technologies;
- processes of diffusion of such technologies to the developing world;
- the impact of such technologies on income, employment and environment;
- the political dynamics of technological transfer.

The series is a pioneering attempt at placing technology policies at the heart of national and international strategies for development. This is likely to prove crucial in the globalized market, for the competitiveness and sustainable growth of poorer nations.

TECHNOLOGY, MARKET STRUCTURE AND INTERNATIONALIZATION

Issues and Policies for Developing Countries

Nagesh Kumar and N.S. Siddharthan

London and New York

INTECH

Institute for New Technologies

Published in association with the UNU Press

First published 1997
by Routledge
11 New Fetter Lane, London EC4P 4EE
Simultaneously published in the USA and Canada
by Routledge
29 West 35th Street, New York, NY 10001
© 1997 UNU/INTECH

Typeset in Times by Routledge
Printed and bound in Great Britain by
Redwood Books, Trowbridge, Wiltshire

British Library Cataloguing in Publication Data
A catalogue record for this book is available from the British Library

Library of Congress Cataloguing in Publication Data
Nagesh, Kumar.
Technology, market structure and internationalization : issues and
policies for developing countries / Nagesh Kumar and N.S. Siddharthan.
Includes bibliographical references and index.
1. Technological innovations–Economic aspects–Developing countries.
2. Technology transfer–Developing countries. 3. Technology and
state–Developing countries. 4. Competition, International. I.
Siddharthan, N.S. II. Title.
HC59.72.T4N34 1997
338'.064'091724–dc21 :97–7415

ISBN 0–415–16925–9

CONTENTS

Part II Technology and market structure

Part III Technology, trade and multinational enterprises

TABLES

PREFACE

This book was conceived in 1992 when both of us were working in New Delhi, and preliminary drafts of some chapters were written then. However, Kumar moved to UNU/INTECH, in Maastricht, the Netherlands, in early 1993 and the compulsions of settling down in a new place demanded that the book project be put on the so-called 'back burner' for a while. It could only be returned to intermittently in the course of 1994 and much of the work was done in 1995/6. The passage of time also allowed us to rethink the book's scope and objectives. Initially our primary objective was to synthesize our work of the past years, some of which was joint, and put it in a perspective to derive policy implications. Gradually the scope of the book evolved from this narrow objective to one attempting to provide a developing country perspective on economic analysis of technology, especially in the industrial organization literature. In the current age of globalization, however, a closed economy model of industrial organization is hardly appropriate. Hence, implications and interface of technology with opening up of the economies to trade, foreign direct investment and external technology flows were brought in to the last part of the book. Finally, the emerging trends in the global economy define the external environment for the process of local technological capability building in any country by shaping the constraints, opportunities and necessitating special responses. This became the focus of Part I of the book.

In terms of the division of labour between us, Kumar prepared initial drafts of Chapters 1, 2, 3, 7, 8 and parts of 9; and Siddharthan, of Chapters 4, 5, 6 and parts of 9. However, we have commented on and revised each other's drafts so extensively that both of us share equally the responsibility for the views expressed and for the errors and omissions in the end product.

In the course of writing this book, we have accumulated debt to several colleagues and friends. Kumar wishes to acknowledge his appreciation of Professor Charles Cooper, Director, UNU/INTECH, for the encouragement and support to the project ever since he moved to UNU/INTECH, but for which it would have been difficult to complete the book. The book has also drawn upon the work done as a part of the UNU/INTECH research project on Foreign Direct Investment, Technology Transfer and Export-Orientation in Developing Countries directed by Kumar. Colleagues at UNU/INTECH, especially Professor Swasti Mitter and Dr Ludovico Alcorta, generously spared their time for reading the drafts, and offered comments and advice. Kumar also tried parts of the book in his lectures forming the module on Technology and Industrial Organization for the course-work segment of the MERIT-UNU/INTECH PhD programme 1995/6, and benefited from the feedback. Additional comments were received from Dr Larry Willmore of the United Nations (DESIPA), New York, Professor Norman Girvan of the University of West Indies, Jamaica, and Dr Rakesh Basant of the Indian Institute of Management, Ahmedabad. Siddharthan would like to thank Professors Edward Safarian of Toronto University, George Waardenburg of Erasmus University, and K.L. Krishna of the Delhi School of Economics, for their several helpful comments and suggestions. Both authors wish to thank Professor John Hagedoorn of the University of Maastricht for permitting them to use some copyrighted material.

Finally, we would both like to thank Ms Alexandra van der Poel for her assistance in the compilation of references and the incorporation of corrections in the text.

Nagesh Kumar and N.S. Siddharthan
Maastricht and New Dehli
29 January 1997

1

INTRODUCTION AND OVERVIEW

THE CONTEXT

Technology has received increasing attention in economic literature in the past few decades. The two central assumptions of the neo-classical growth theory, that technological change is exogenous and that the same technological opportunities are available to all countries in the world, have been shed. Technological change has been incorporated endogenously in the new growth theories (Romer, 1986, 1994; Lucas, 1988; Grossman and Helpman, 1991). By specifying technology endogenously, the new theories recognize knowledge or technology as a factor of production in its own right, alongside capital and labour. That helps to rectify the inability of neo-classical theory to explain the failure of poorer countries to catch up with the high-income countries and in providing a possibility of non-diminishing returns to capital as the capital stock grows. The role of technology in determining a country's international trade and hence competitiveness has been emphasized in the neo-technology theories of trade (see, among others, Posner, 1961; Vernon, 1966; Hufbauer, 1966; Krugman, 1979) and subsequent empirical literature (see, for instance, Gruber *et al.*, 1967; Caves *et al.*, 1980; Hughes, 1986; Soete, 1987; Mowery and Rosenburg, 1989). With the global economy becoming more and more open and interdependent with liberalization of international trade and other economic exchanges, international competitiveness and hence technology are currently receiving increasing attention in the trade literature as well as in policy-making. President Clinton and Mr Gore rightly argue in their 1993 statement on *Technology for America's Economic Growth* that 'international competitiveness depends less and less on traditional factors such as access to natural resources and cheap labour. Instead, the new growth industries are knowledge-based. They depend on the continuous generation of new technological innovations and the rapid transformation of these innovations into commercial products the world wants to buy.'

Given its critical role in economic growth and international competitiveness, technology has received important attention in economic policy-making in most industrialized and newly industrializing economies. The national or federal and local governments play an important role in the national innovation systems of these countries (see several country case studies in Nelson, 1993). The aggressive manner in which industrialized country governments have pushed technological activities of national enterprises has been termed a 'technology race' (Roobeek, 1990).

On the other hand, technology does not yet receive due attention in development policy in most developing countries. The relative neglect of technology by developing countries explains the disproportionate and ever widening gap between rich and poor countries in the area of science and technology (see Patel, 1995, for a discussion of the dynamics of the economic and technological gap between nations). While it is true that developing countries can benefit from the global pool of technologies and knowledge by several channels of transfer and diffusion and not reinvent everything themselves, literature has emphasized the need for some capability of their own even to be able effectively to employ technologies available abroad in the process of their development. Furthermore, the limited empirical analysis that has been made for developing country enterprises has found their ability to access international markets to be dependent on their own technological effort even in low and medium technology industries (see, among others, Kumar and Siddharthan, 1994). Cooper (1995) found that the technological capability of some developing countries was the key to their ability to expand exports of increasingly more technologically complex products or to adopt a technological upgrading path of export-expansion. The capability efficiently to employ existing technologies in their development, besides creating some new knowledge for dealing with specific problems, comprises what is termed local technological capability in the developing country context. In other words, the development policy concerning technology in developing countries should aim at building local technological capability (hereafter technological capability). Dahlman *et al.* (1987: 774), after surveying the literature on acquisition of technological capability, conclude that 'the central issue of technological development in developing countries is ... acquiring the capability to use existing technology to produce more efficiently, to establish better production facilities, and to use the experience gained in production and investment to adapt and improve the technology in use'. This book discusses some of the important determinants of, and other factors that impinge on, the process of building technological capability in developing countries in industry.

TECHNOLOGICAL CAPABILITY AND INNOVATION IN DEVELOPING COUNTRIES: DEFINITION, IMPORTANCE AND DETERMINANTS

A significant volume of literature in the 1970s and 1980s has been devoted to the issue of technological capability building in developing countries. Perhaps this was provoked by the relatively successful Korean effort to build technological capability (Westphal *et al.*, 1979; Cooper, 1980; Bell *et al.*, 1982; Dahlman, 1984; Fransman, 1984, 1986; Katz, 1984; Lall, 1984, 1987; Langdon, 1984; Stewart, 1984; Dahlman *et al.*, 1987; Amsden, 1989; Enos, 1991, among others). Stewart (1984: 81) defines indigenous technological capability as the capacity to create, adapt and modify technology thus including in it local adaptation and development of technology already known elsewhere as well as creation of some completely new technology.

The literature has also emphasized the importance of technological capability even for importing technology and applying it effectively. For instance, Pack and Westphal (1986: 121), against the background of the imperfectly competitive nature of technology markets, note that the acquisition of domestic technological capability may result in improved terms for technology purchases by increasing local capability to evaluate the commercial value of the proposed license and by providing knowledge of a greater range of suppliers. Dahlman (1984: 329) observes that indigenous technological capability is needed not only to modify, adapt and improve the original technology but also for screening and monitoring foreign technological advances and for incorporating some of them for local use. Stewart (1984) finds additional reasons for developing countries trying to establish indigenous technological capability. Besides using imported technology efficiently and getting an edge in bargaining for technology transactions, this capability helps 'to create technology with appropriate characteristics', and because of the cumulative nature of learning effects, doing it yourself may eventually create a 'dynamic comparative advantage in more sophisticated and often more remunerative lines of production'. The latter is quite similar to what comprises the technological upgrading path described by Cooper (1995).

Nature of technological capability

Enos (1991) identifies three fundamental components of technological capability: individuals with inclination, training and experience; institutions, e.g. a firm, a cooperative or an agency, within which individuals with different talents assemble; and most importantly, a common purpose or objective without which the first two would remain unproductive. Building technological capability requires a massive effort in developing human resources (individuals) and institutions and in defining their purpose. Dahlman *et al.* (1987: 759), for instance, concluded from their survey that, although experience is important, technological capability is not acquired merely from experience. It comes from a conscious effort in monitoring and keeping track of developments throughout the world, accumulation of added skills, and responding to new pressures and opportunities.

The other characteristic that needs emphasis is the dynamic and continuous nature of the effort to build local technological capability. Technological capability is a relative concept and is judged with respect to global standards. The global technology frontier keeps moving forward continuously and indeed has moved very rapidly since the evolution of new core technologies such as microelectronics, information technologies and biotechnologies. Countries encounter varying degrees of difficulty in building up technological capability in different industrial sectors because of the nature and rate of change of the underlying technology. Also, capability in different industries may have different spillovers and linkages for learning in related sectors. Hence, sequencing and prioritizing could be an important consideration for policy.

Another aspect that has been emphasized in the literature is the evolution of technological capability in successive stages which requires an increasing level of technological mastery of the knowledge involved in a particular economic activity. Lall (1987), for instance, has defined five successive stages of technological capability. These are: (a) the ability to make efficient pre-investment choices such as the ability to define the project specifications and select a source of technology; (b) actual project execution; (c) the ability to operate a plant which may include capability to carry out troubleshooting and incorporate some adaptations; (d) the ability to make technological improvements and design new processes and products: and finally, (e) transfer of technology to other firms. By the time a firm reaches the last stage in its technological evolution, it would be competing in the global market as a source of products and technology. Therefore the ability to compete globally with product and process innovations is the highest stage of technological capability building at the enterprise level. Gaining mastery of technologies imported by individual firms is necessary but not a sufficient condition for sustaining the comparative advantage of a nation. The latter involves a more complex process of continual technological upgrading of products and processes within industries, entry into progressively more complex new activities, and increasing local inputs and linkages even for more difficult manufacturing tasks (Lall, 1995: 111–12).

Actors in technological capability building and innovation

The term 'national innovation system' has been recently incorporated into the literature to define the institutional set-up that results in technological innovations – technological capability in a developing countries context (see Lundvall, 1992; Nelson, 1993). Nelson (1993: 4) defines the system as a set of institutions whose interactions determine the innovative performance of national firms. Lundvall (1992: 12) is more elaborate, while covering in his broad definition 'all parts and aspects of the economic structure and the institutional set-up affecting learning as well as searching and exploring the production system, the marketing system and system of finance'. Both Lundvall and Nelson would include firms, industrial research laboratories, government laboratories and universities and other institutions of higher education among the major institutional actors in the national innovation system.

It seems to be in order to classify the important actors in building techno-logical capability into two broad groups: government and business enterprises; although sometimes government and the business sector work together in creating some institutional infrastructure. The government plays an important role in building local capability through several means, e.g. by generating a skilled manpower base with the creation of an educational infrastructure which is a crucial prerequisite, by defining goals for business enterprises with respect to technological capability and providing for their fulfilment with an enabling policy framework, by creating an institutional infrastructure for technology development such as setting up common facility centres (e.g. testing facilities, tool room centres, etc.), by encour-aging, protecting and supporting local technological development in enterprises through different policy instruments, and by funding and support for basic and fundamental research which might not be taken up by enterprises.

Business enterprises (including those owned partly or wholly by govern-ments) are the key actors in technological capability building because they have the prospect of considerable learning in the process of setting up a manufacturing plant, its day-to-day running and replicating, opportunities for absorbing knowledge from their suppliers in the process of adapting the products or processes to local environment or to customer requirements, keeping track of technological developments world-wide in their lines of activity and keeping themselves up to date. They are also the ones who actu-ally apply technological capability or new knowledge in production processes and thus exploit its economic potential. In other words the poten-tial of knowledge or technology for economic growth and competitiveness is realized when that knowledge is applied by enterprises in their economic activities. National enterprises in certain industries may contribute more to the local technological capability than those in other industries. For instance, national firms in certain industries, i.e. machinery manufacturers and consultancy and design engineering firms, play a more important role in local technological capability because of their ability to diffuse technology in other sectors of the economy by supply of equipment incorporating new knowledge (see, among others, Kumar and Waslekar, 1994 for a discussion of design engineering services in developing countries).

A major component of the policy to build local technological capability, therefore, is encouragement of technological effort and learning in firms. Hence, an analysis of factors that determine the technological activities of firms assumes importance in the context of building local technological capability.

Determinants of technological effort of enterprises: a framework of analysis

A rather voluminous stream of literature on innovation has explored the factors influencing the technological effort or innovative activity of enterprises. A major preoccupation of this stream of literature has been with verifying the hypotheses of the positive effect of firm size and market structure on innovation inspired by Schumpeter (1942) and a number of neo-Schumpeterian contributions including Nelson and Winter (1982) (see, among others, Hay and Morris, 1991; Cohen, 1995, for recent reviews of the literature). Subsequent studies have emphasized the importance of industry characteristics such as technological opportunities (Scherer, 1965), demand (Schmookler, 1962) and appropriability conditions in determining the technological effort of enterprises. Furthermore, as emphasized in the previous section, governments play an important role in determining innovation and technological effort of business enterprises by several direct and indirect means, although the empirical studies in the industrial organization stream of literature have seldom examined the role of these policies (see Mayer-Krahmer, 1990, for an attempt to examine the role of public policies in determining R&D investment in Germany). For instance, a government's policy with respect to the protection of intellectual property influences the nature and magnitude of innovative activity, and policies with respect to technology purchase from abroad affect the strategy of local enterprises with respect to sourcing of technology whether from own R&D or purchases. Provision of technological infrastructure, subsidies and tax concessions, subsidized financing and venture capital, among other policies, may encourage enterprises to undertake innovative activity. The provision of technological infrastructure by governments could be of critical importance, especially in developing countries' efforts to develop some local capability in new core technologies, as will be illustrated in Chapter 3 with a case study of biotechnology.

Besides the domestic factors such as market structure, demand or appropriability, the technological effort of firms could be affected in a significant manner by the external linkages of the enterprise. These linkages include the extent and nature of technology imports, the controlling foreign ownership and affiliation with multinational enterprises (MNEs) (Caves *et al.*, 1980). With the growing internationalization and globalization of businesses in the recent years, these links are becoming increasingly more important and visible with time. The decision about the location of innovative activity of

MNEs is taken at the corporate headquarters in tune with several strategic considerations. Hence, the technological effort of MNE affiliates may be different from that of unaffiliated local firms (see, among others, Kumar, 1991). Purchases of technology from abroad may substitute the need for innovation or may require further technological effort for the adaptation and assimilation of borrowed technology. Furthermore, the market-orientation, i.e. the exposure to the international market of a firm, may also have an influence on its technological effort as much as technological activities may affect the international competitiveness, and hence the international market presence, of the firm itself (see, among others, Mansfield *et al.*, 1979; Hughes, 1986; Kumar and Saqib, 1996).

Finally, a firm's technological activities are conducted in an environment shaped not only by the national government's policies and institutional structure but increasingly also by emerging economic, institutional and technological trends in the global economy. For instance, the current trend of strengthening and harmonization of intellectual property world-wide has the prospect of affecting the technological effort of many enterprises in developing countries where most of the changes with respect to the rules will take place. Similarly, the restructuring of businesses world-wide sparked by the emergence of regional trading blocs may also affect the locus of technological activities among other parameters.

THIS BOOK: OBJECTIVES, STRUCTURE AND AN OVERVIEW OF CONCLUSIONS AND POLICY IMPLICATIONS

The subject matter of this book relates to some of the factors that reflect the technological activities of firms, especially in a developing country setting, and policy responses that arise from this discussion. As observed earlier, an enormous volume of literature has appeared in recent years empirically testing the neo-Schumpeterian propositions and other determinants of innovation (see Cohen, 1995, for a most up-to-date survey of the literature). However, the bulk of the literature is industrialized country based. Although much is to be learned from the innovation studies on industrialized economies for technology policy formulation in developing countries (Cooper, 1991, 1994), several differences in a developing country's situation may affect the outcome of policies. For instance, the nature of technological effort or innovative activity of enterprises in developing countries is generally different from that of their industrialized counterparts. The former may comprise more adaptations of given products and processes to local situations, downscaling of processes, indigenization of raw materials, and subsequently technological updating, while innovation in the industrialized country enterprises might be more creative or product development oriented. This implies that, unlike technological opportunities that gear innovations of industrialized country enterprises, opportunities for adaptations may be more relevant factors for explaining the technological effort of developing country enterprises (Kumar and Saqib, 1996). Also, the nature of the interface between technology imports and local technological effort may differ depending upon the initial absorptive capacity, among other factors. Finally, as Cooper (1991: 15) has pointed out, the Arrowian learning processes that are assumed to be automatic in an industrialized country context may often fail to take place in developing country settings without 'a conscious allocation of resources within the firm' and 'appropriate external institutional conditions'. 'Learning probably breaks down in developing countries more than in industrialised countries.' These differences and others have to be kept in mind while generalizing the findings obtained for industrialized country samples and applying them to developing countries.

In recent years there have been a number of studies empirically explaining the innovative activity of developing country enterprises. These studies, however, have not been integrated in recent surveys of the literature; for instance, Kamien and Schwartz, 1982; Cohen and Levin, 1989; Hay and Morris, 1991; Cohen, 1995, hardly list any developing country based study. In other words, little attempt has been made to provide a coherent treatment of the empirical determinants of the technological effort of enterprises from the perspective of developing countries. This book attempts to fill this gap in the literature. The three parts of the book discuss trends in the global economic environment with implications for technological effort in developing countries, empirical literature on the neo-Schumpeterian determinants of technological activities, and the interface between technological effort of enterprises and external economic links such as technology imports, affiliations with MNEs, and international trade. More specific objectives of the book will become clear from the structure described in the next section. In view of its focus on technological effort at the enterprise level, the industrial organization framework of economic analysis has been considered appropriate for most of the discussion.

Chapter layout and an overview of policy implications

The main subject matter of the book has been classified into three parts.

Part 1 deals with some of the emerging trends in the global economic environment, especially those that have implications for building technological capability in developing countries. Among other trends it discusses the emergence of new technologies and other related developments such as those relating to technological protectionism and trade negotiations and specific policy responses needed at the government level in developing countries in view of the special problems they pose for building capabilities in these countries. It is demonstrated with the help of a case study of biotechnology in which some developing countries tried to establish a certain capability and had some success in creating an institutional infrastructure for promoting technological effort at the enterprises level. Chapter 2 specifically discusses the emerging economic trends of global and regional economic integration and their implications for developing countries' technological effort. It discusses the emergence of new technologies and the special problems that it raises for capability building in developing countries. It also discusses the recent trends in technological protectionism in industrialized countries, new international regimes for intellectual property protection, and the emerging regime for international investments and technology transfers and their implications for capability building in developing countries. It then reviews the implications of the Bank-Fund administered structural adjustment programmes undertaken by many developing countries for their technological effort. Chapter 2 concludes with policy implications which emphasize an important role for governmental intervention in building technological capabilities in developing countries. The form that governmental intervention takes would vary from country to country, depending among other factors upon the country's characteristics such as size, goals of development policy, skill base and existence and maturity of local institutions and entrepreneurship.

Chapter 3 picks up the thread from a discussion in Chapter 2 of the evolution of new technologies which raises special problems for building technological capability. This is highlighted with a case study of the biotechnology industry in Chapter 3. It highlights the enormous development potential of biotechnologies that exists in different areas. The chapter goes on to discuss those emerging trends in global biotechnology industry which tend to affect adversely the diffusion of these technologies to developing countries. It then reviews the recent attempts by a number of developing country governments to build an institutional infrastructure in their countries to harness the potential of biotechnology for solving their specific problems by creating local technological capability and expertise in this area. The programmes of international cooperation, including mutual cooperation, and their potential are also reviewed. The chapter concludes on a more optimistic note than did the previous one on the prospects of building some technological capability in developing countries in new core technologies despite other adverse trends, providing that governments take the initiative to build the appropriate institutional infrastructure for technology development – as did the ones covered in the case studies reviewed. (However, these case studies concentrated on relatively more successful cases.)

Part 2 focuses on neo-Schumpeterian and other determinants of the technological effort of enterprises dealt with in the industrial organization literature. Chapter 4 deals with firm size and technological activity. The Schumpeterian and neo-Schumpeterian (or evolutionary theory) propositions with respect to the role of firm size are discussed. The chapter then reviews the empirical literature, especially the recent studies from developing countries and their policy implications. The general conclusion of the empirical studies on firm size and formal technological effort summarized in the chapter suggests that firm size tends to affect the probability of a firm having an R&D laboratory and the intensity of R&D expenditure in a positive manner in developing countries, in contrast to the somewhat inconclusive finding reached by industrialized country literature. Given the economies of scale in R&D, the productivity of technological effort of larger firms may be higher because of the larger scale of their R&D. Therefore the evidence would tend to support policies that encourage the larger national enterprises to take a greater role in building technological capabilities of a nation. While the technological activities of small and medium enterprises are important and should be encouraged especially in new technologies, it is the technological activities of large national enterprises that can make a visible difference to the national technological capabilities. Japan and Korea were able to build highly competitive technological capabilities by encouraging the technological activities of their large enterprises. The national technological capabilities in different sectors of different countries are indeed reflected in the relative capabilities of their respective national champions. It may be fruitful for developing countries to focus their efforts on building technological capability in select areas by encouraging large national enterprises to build their own technological capabilities. This would enable them to make increasingly independent technological choices and to expand. Vertical inter-firm linkages between larger enterprises and smaller firms may be encouraged in order to allow for diffusion of technology through traditional vendor–customer links.

Chapter 5 deals with the role of the second Schumpeterian factor, i.e. market structure, and other determinants of technological effort such as appropriability and technological opportunities in determining the technological effort. The chapter reviews the empirical literature on these factors, especially from developing countries. It is now widely recognized that the market structure and innovation relationship may be subject to a simultaneity problem in that it may also run from innovation to market structure. From the evidence reviewed it appears that neither highly competitive market structures nor monopoly are conducive to technological innovations. Market structures with a few sellers and a few buyers and with a constant threat of entry may be more appropriate for promoting a rivalry based on innovation among them and hence may spur technological effort under certain conditions. This competition policy has a role to play by preventing the build-up of excessive monopoly power of certain enterprises and ensuring a level playing-field for different firms. Neither the theoretical nor the empirical literature provide a strong justification for intellectual property rights as an important determinant of innovative activity except in a few industries. Strong intellectual property protection also has the propensity to affect the technological activities of a number of enterprises adversely by stifling the flow of spillovers from the R&D of other firms. In developing countries, strong intellectual property protection might affect the technological effort of enterprises and hence the process of capability building adversely by curtailing the 'opportunities for adaptation'.

Chapter 6 discusses the treatment in the theoretical and empirical literature of the role that technological activities play in determining industry and firm profitability and growth. The chapter explores the explanation for the inability of empirical studies fully to capture the role that technology plays in determining different parameters of performance. We discuss the conceptual and empirical explanations of the poor performance of the technology factor in the empirical literature and review recent studies that confirmed its role in determining industry and corporate profitability and growth. The studies also reported high rates of return on R&D and other forms of technological effort. Chapter 6 then observes that, despite such high returns, enterprises in developing countries may not be willing to invest in R&D activity because of high risk, economies of scale, lack of infrastructure, non-availability of finance, etc. Hence, governments have an important promotional role to play in inducing enterprises to undertake R&D.

Part 3 extends the discussion to include the interaction of innovative activity or technological effort of enterprises with their foreign linkages. The interactions between technology imports and their mode, international trade, market structures and local technological effort are explored in the three chapters that constitute this part of the book. Chapter 7 discusses the interaction between technology, market structure and multinational affiliation or foreign ownership of industries. It first summarizes the contemporary theory of internationalization of firms that has been used for analysing the determinants of foreign direct investment (FDI) and technology transfers across countries, industries and over time in numerous studies. The evidence from these studies is reviewed with a view to derive policy implications. It then discusses the theoretical and empirical issues concerning the impact of MNE operations on host country market structures. The analysis of this chapter suggests that excessive trade liberalization by developing countries may prompt MNEs to export to them rather than produce locally as liberalization dilutes the intensity of the main locational advantage, i.e. the protection accorded to local industries by the host governments. Similarly, liberalization of foreign direct investment codes may change the balance between FDI and licensing in favour of the former as a mode of local production. FDI inflows to developing countries have been highly concentrated in a handful of such countries and have been determined primarily by the market size, growth rates, prosperity, urbanization, quality of infrastructure and other such considerations more than by the host country incentives and other policies. MNE operations tend to raise barriers to entry for new firms and hence affect the levels of competition in host economies adversely. With their access to global brand names and the other resources of their parents, MNE affiliates are able to corner the upper end of the markets in their respective product lines, leaving the usually more competitive lower ends for local firms. In a significant number of cases, MNE entry takes the form of acquisition of a domestic competitor. Furthermore, international mergers and acquisitions also affect the market structures in the host countries of MNEs involved. Liberalization of policy towards FDI should be accompanied by stronger competition or anti-trust policies. In developing countries the competition policy need not be regulatory alone; it could be proactive as well. For instance, it could contribute to the creation of a level playing-field for local enterprises by assisting them in building strong national brands and technological capabilities. Finally, the chapter touches upon an important development of recent years, the internationalization of developing country enterprises and the evolution of outward FDI flows from developing countries. In so far as overseas investments of national enterprises contribute to their market access in the host countries, these investments may be supported by home governments. Developing country enterprises are also emerging as promising sources of FDI and technology for the relatively less developed countries which are neglected by Western enterprises.

Chapter 8 deals with the interaction between technology, international trade and multinational enterprises. It highlights the importance attached by the theoretical and empirical literature to technological effort in determining the international competitiveness of enterprises and nations, including the recent extensions of the technology theories of trade to explain the role of technology in determining trade in the developing country context. The chapter then draws attention to a possible simultaneity problem that characterizes the export and technology relationship. Attention is then turned to the role of MNEs in export expansion in developing countries. The main explanation for the diverging contribution of MNEs to the expansion of host country exports, as observed by studies, is to be found in the varying ability of countries to attract export-oriented or export platform FDI. The export-oriented FDI has been found to be a special type of FDI determined by factors different from those that determine the domestic market oriented FDI inflows. These flows are highly concentrated in a few countries that are able to offer better industrial infrastructure and capability in addition to low cost labour, and offer a potential to relatively less developed countries for expanding their manufactured exports. Finally, the chapter deals with a related phenomenon, that of intra-firm trade, which has grown in importance over the past few decades and accounts for a considerable proportion of global trade. Intra-firm trade results from the vertical integration of affiliates of MNEs in the process of fragmentation of production across the world. The empirical literature reviewed has shown that intra-firm trade predominates technology and skill intensive branches of industries. Therefore export-oriented FDI would be a principal means of tapping the market access of MNEs by developing countries in skill and technology intensive industries. In the case of more standardized and mature industries, such as textiles and the manufacture of garments and leather goods, subcontracting of production without controlling affiliations of MNEs may also be a possible means of expanding manufactured exports.

Chapter 9 examines the issues concerning the interface between technology imports and domestic technological capability building in developing countries. The relationship between technology imports and local R&D or technological effort is found to be rather complex, depending upon a number of factors. One factor that was highlighted by the discussion and which has policy implications is the mode of technology imports. Evidence suggests that, under some conditions, technology imports unaccompanied by ownership and management may be more efficient from the point of view of local technological capability building than those accompanied by foreign ownership. Numerous instances are now available of East Asian enterprises importing technology unaccompanied by ownership and control and gradually becoming internationally competitive with further technological effort. The strategy of importing technology through contractual modes could, however, succeed in countries having high absorptive capacity. Second, while an infant industry type of protection to local technologies against imported technologies is desirable, a too-restrictive policy on technology imports tends to choke any technological dynamism of local enterprises by creating a virtual monopoly situation for the first importers. It might also restrict the flow of knowledge to the country. A tax on technology imports may be a more effective means of providing protection to local technology than discretionary barriers which tend to be bureaucratic. Technology imports can also contribute to the technological capability building in the host country through spillovers of knowledge to other domestic firms. The evidence on knowledge spillovers from foreign direct investment to their local counterparts in the host economy suggests that local enterprises that have some technological strength generally benefit from the 'competitive spur' provided by the entry of a foreign competitor, while technologically weak national firms tend to be affected adversely by foreign entry. Therefore governments in developing countries tend to take a phased approach to liberalization of their markets to MNEs to provide weaker local enterprises enough time to develop some capabilities and strength. FDI and technology imports could also have considerable spillovers of knowledge to the host economy and to other national firms. Studies show that these spillovers have been facilitated by a somewhat softer regime of intellectual property protection. The host governments may also adopt complementary policies to promote these spillovers.

Part I

THE EXTERNAL ENVIRONMENT FOR BUILDING TECHNOLOGICAL CAPABILITY

This part discusses some trends in global economy that have implications for the attempt of developing countries to build their local technological capabilities and their place in the international division of labour. These trends include global and regional economic integration, technological protectionism, emergence of new technologies, emerging international regimes for intellectual property protection and international investments. It also touches upon some trends in developing country policies such as that of structural adjustment and liberalization for their own effort to build local technological capability. These trends, most of which are external to the developing countries' own policies, require a response from their governments. This is illustrated further in Chapter 3 with the help of a case study of biotechnology, which shows that its tremendous development potential could remain unexploited unless local technological capabilities are built up in developing countries, which in turn are critically dependent upon their governments' initiatives in infrastructure development.

2

GLOBALIZATION, NEW TECHNOLOGIES AND THE URUGUAY ROUND

Changed international context for the development of local capability in developing countries

INTRODUCTION

Developing countries cannot build industrial and technological capabilities in isolation from the rest of the world. The external economic, technological and political environment affects the process of capability building in a country in a substantial manner. The capability, indeed, is defined in a relative sense and is judged with respect to the global standards.

The international context for capability building has altered considerably over the past two decades due to several economic, financial, technological and institutional changes. This has implications for the process of capability building in developing countries. This chapter summarizes the contours of these trends emerging in the global economy and their implications for the process of development of local capabilities in developing countries. The rest of the chapter is organized as follows. The next section summarizes the recent trends in the growth of international transactions in goods and services that point to an increased economic integration across the world economy. Many of these trends actually reflect the deep international economic integration that has taken place over the past five years or more in the frameworks of regional trading blocs, e.g. the Single Market Plan of the European Union and the North American Free Trade Area (NAFTA). The implications of these trading blocs for developing countries are summarized in the following section. The next section discusses the evolution of new core technologies having very widespread applications and the special problems they pose for the building capabilities of developing countries. After this, the trends in governmental intervention in the industrialized countries in the area of technologies are discussed. The next two sections review the implications of new international rules for the protection of intellectual property, and of the recent initiatives to establish international rules on international investments and hence, transfer of technology. The penultimate section discusses the trends in scientific and technological activity in developing countries and the implications of structural adjustment programmes for them, and the chapter concludes with some observations for policies.

GLOBAL ECONOMIC INTEGRATION

One of the most notable trends in global economy has been its increasing economic integration since the mid-1980s. The world economy has witnessed a growing internationalization since then which is reflected in terms of the rising share of international trade and foreign direct investment (FDI) outflows. Table 2.1 shows that the average annual growth rate of world merchandizing trade during the second half of the 1980s nearly doubled that of the world output. FDI outflows expanded at an annual rate of 29 per cent during the last five years of the last decade and at 10 per cent over the first five years of the 1990s, climbing to a level of US$318 billion in 1995. Liberalization of international trade in services was another important development of the late 1980s. As a result, world trade in commercial services has expanded at the average rate of nearly 22 per cent. A cumulative effect of these trends has been to make the world economy far more integrated economically in the 1990s than before.

The growing magnitude of FDI is actually a reflection of the growth of foreign production. A considerable part of production within multinational enterprises takes place as globally integrated production where production units located in different parts of the world are vertically integrated. This globalization of production is made possible by recent advances in manufacturing technologies that enable fragmentation of production processes, by improvement in transportation technologies, e.g. containerization that makes transportation easier and cheaper, and new information and communication technologies that make coordination of production units at different locations easier.

Liberalization of international trade in services has become an established trend. The financial services were internationalized in a big way in the late 1980s. The inflows of portfolio equity capital to developing countries which were negligible till the mid-1980s expanded to reach nearly US$47 billion in 1993 and were of the order of $40 billion in 1994. The expansion

Table 2.1 Average annual growth rates of global economic indicators, 1975–95

Indicator	1971–85	1986–90	1991–5
World output	3.2	3.3	1.76
World merchandise trade	3.7	6.1	6.14
World FDI outflows	−0.5*	29.0	10.15
World trade in commercial services	1.2*	21.7	6.00 †

* for 1980–5; † for 1991–3
Source: compiled from World Bank and UNCTAD sources

of international trade in financial services was facilitated by the deregulation of financial markets world-wide and new information technologies. It has diminished the power of central banks to control exchange rates.

Liberalization was hardly confined to trade in financial services alone. A large number of business services, such as banking, insurance, advertising, accounting, communications, media, car rental and catering services, have become increasingly internationalized during the late 1980s. The internationalization of these services is highly visible and also affects consumption and demand patterns, especially in media and advertising services. These developments tend to strengthen the competitive edge of global corporations over that of national enterprises by providing greater visibility and exposure to their products and brand names world-wide.

REGIONAL ECONOMIC INTEGRATION

Another major trend of the recent period has been the formation of regional trading blocs among the industrialized countries. The EC countries restructured themselves to form the Single European Market (SEM) in 1992 which culminated in an expanded economic and political European Union (EU). The North American countries, i.e. the US, Canada and Mexico, have formed the North American Free Trade Area (NAFTA). These trading blocs represent cross-national integration of a deep nature between the participating countries. For the non-participating countries, however, these trading blocs pose a threat of trade diversion because of discrimination against extra-regional supplies and the threat of increased protectionism and restrictions. This integration affects the position of developing countries in the international division of labour in a significant manner, as shown here in the case of the SEM.

The pan-European rationalization of production and marketing and corporate restructuring sparked by the SEM will enable the EU enterprises to reap economies of scale, making them more competitive. The EU enterprises will also gain competitiveness by moving production to cheaper wage locations within the customs union, e.g. Spain, Portugal and Greece. The increased competitiveness of the EU supplies coupled with the threat of discrimination against non-EU goods by means of common external tariffs suggest that exports to the EU would be adversely affected. With the SEM, the EU is expected to be more self-reliant, thus affecting imports from its trading partners adversely. The trade diversion for developing countries is expected to be greatest for the low-value, undifferentiated and highly price elastic goods such as textiles, clothing, footwear, leather goods, electronic components, metals and chemicals (Page, 1991). Furthermore, the EU has granted special and preferential access to its market to neighbouring Mediterranean and East European countries. These countries are increasingly substituting low income developing countries for relocation of production initially meant for developing countries because of their special access to the EU market. With the economic reforms, the Eastern and Central European countries are becoming integrated into the world economy. This has two implications for developing countries. First, these Eastern and Central European countries are increasingly competing with developing countries in attracting FDI inflows. In the past few years they have received considerable amounts of FDI inflow. Second, these countries have signed agreements with the EU providing for free trade, economic and technical cooperation and financial assistance. They are, therefore, becoming integrated with the EU economies as convenient backyards with an abundant supply of low-wage labour. Because of their special access to the EU market, Central and Eastern European countries are substituting for the low-income developing countries as bases for export platform production for the EU market (Kumar, 1994c). The emergence of new organizational techniques such as just-in-time inventory systems adds further to the attractiveness of these backyards because of their geographical proximity (Kaplinsky, 1991). In other words, preferential access to the trading blocs has become an important determinant of international competitiveness in recent years.

EMERGENCE OF NEW CORE TECHNOLOGIES AND CAPABILITY BUILDING IN DEVELOPING COUNTRIES

The emergence of new technologies such as microelectronics, biotechnology and new materials, based on recent advances in basic sciences, is having important implications for the position of developing countries in the global technological order. These technologies find application in a wide array of industries and sectors of the economy and hence their mastery and control is increasingly becoming a major determinant of international competitiveness (Mody and Wheeler, 1990). Roobeek (1990) has used the expression 'technology web' to indicate the all-pervasive nature of these technologies. Advances in microelectronics, for instance, have not only given increasingly more efficient computers but also computer aided manufacture (CAM), which finds application in virtually every major sector of manufacturing, from textiles and garment making to all types of processing industries such as food, chemicals, drugs, cement and so on. Flexible manufacturing systems result in enormous economies of scope and have considerably enhanced the scope and possibilities for automation. Computer aided design (CAD) is revolutionizing the engineering industry at large, while applications of computers and digital equipment have changed the services industries such as telecommunications, banking, transport, medicine and health in a dramatic manner.

Biotechnologies are having a major impact on agriculture, stock-breeding and animal husbandry, human and veterinary health care, the pharmaceutical industry, the chemical industry, the food processing and beverages industry, the energy sector and waste treatment. Similarly the sectors of applications of new materials include telecommunications, computers and semiconductors, aerospace and defence, machinery and motors, building and construction, automobiles and transport, chemicals, energy and so on. Furthermore, all three new technologies are reinforcing one another. For instance, microelectronics-based equipment is critical for biotechnology research, biotechnology feeds into the development of new materials, and biotechnology and new materials have important synergies with microelectronics. There are also overlaps in the applications of these technologies. A number of industries are affected by more than one new technology.

Recognizing the importance and potential of the new core technologies, all major corporations in the industrialized world have increasingly geared their activities in the direction of these core technologies. This has been achieved either through further specialization by companies already in the related areas, or by increasing diversification into related areas (see Tulder and Junne, 1988, for an illustration of the strategies of European corporations). As a result the R&D activity in these technologies is heavily concentrated in the triad nations, USA, the EC and Japan. Even though the innovative activity in these technologies is not subject to economies of scale and much of it has actually originated, at least in the US, in small venture capital firms, a handful of large MNEs have come to control much of the knowledge through mergers, acquisitions and strategic alliances besides R&D spending.

An indication of the increasing concentration of activities of the major corporations in these technologies can be had from an analysis of the sectoral distribution of nearly four thousand strategic alliances entered into by the major corporations during the 1980s all over the world and compiled in the MERIT-CATI database. This analysis, summarized in Table 2.2, shows that over 75 per cent of these alliances related to new technologies. The alliances covered in the database include inter-firm agreements that contain some arrangements for transferring technology or research between independent partners which are not connected through majority ownership, such as joint research pacts, second-sourcing and licensing agreements and research corporations (see Hagedoorn and Schakenraad, 1991). The share of new technologies is even higher among alliances oriented to technology sharing, joint R&D, and other innovation-related pacts, and shows a rising trend from the early 1980s to the second half of the decade. It is evident that over 80 per cent of the technology-oriented strategic alliances concerned the new technologies.

In view of their wide ranging applications, access to these technologies is increasingly becoming crucial to international competitiveness.

Table 2.2 Distribution of international strategic alliances, 1980–9

Technology/ sector	Technology/ R&D/ innovation-oriented alliances		Marketing/ production-oriented alliances		All alliances
	1980–4 (%)	1985–9 (%)	1980–4 (%)	1985–9 (%)	1980–9 (%)
Biotechnology	222 (27.82)	456 (27.74)	30 (5.61)	78 (9.56)	786 (20.72)
New materials	58 (7.27)	224 (13.62)	55 (10.28)	80 (9.80)	417 (10.99)
Information technology	324 (40.60)	658 (40.02)	280 (52.34)	389 (47.67)	1651 (43.53)
Other technologies	194 (24.31)	306 (18.61)	170 (31.77)	269 (32.96)	939 (24.75)
All technologies	798 (100)	1644 (100)	535 (100)	816 (100)	3793 (100)

Source: compiled from Hagedoorn and Schakenraad (1991): part 2, Appendices III and IV, pp. 72–5

Besides, each of these core technologies has a tremendous developmental potential and could be a valuable ally to the developing countries in fighting poverty, unemployment, disease, environmental pollution and ecological damage, and help in increasing the efficiency and productivity in several activities, besides saving energy and other resources. Some illustrations from biotechnology are provided later in this book. Hence, developing countries need to build capabilities in these technologies to be able to apply them in their economic activities. However, the process of building capabilities in these technologies poses special problems. First, they are highly skill intensive in nature. The scarcity of human skills in most developing countries tends to be a constraint for the building of capability in these technologies and their widespread diffusion. Second, the technology frontier in these technologies is moving at a rapid pace, not allowing standardization. This creates special problems for countries that are trying to catch up, as they have to keep trying to catch up for ever. Third, a few large international oligopolies are dominating each of these technologies as a result of the increasing commercialization of R&D activity, corporate concentration with a large number of mergers and amalgamations, and a complicated web of strategic alliances between large corporations. Tuldar and Junne (1988), for instance, have observed a high concentration of national R&D expenditure in a few large corporations in most of the industrialized countries. As much as 81 per cent of all Swiss national R&D expenditure in 1983 was accounted for by four companies: Ciba-Geigy, Hoffman-La Roche, BBC and Sandoz; Philips, Shell, Akzo, and Unilever accounted for 69 per cent of Dutch R&D expenditure; Siemens, Bayer, Hoechst, Daimler and VW accounted for 22 per cent of German R&D expenditure; GM, IBM, AT&T, Ford and United Technologies accounted for 12 per cent of US R&D expenditure; and so on (Tuldar and Junne, 1988: Table 6.5).

An indication of the high concentration of new technologies in industrialized countries and the marginalization of developing countries can be had from the international distribution of strategic alliances covered by the MERIT-CATI database. Table 2.3 shows that as many as 95 per cent of these alliances are entered into between enterprises from the industrialized countries, with the US, Europe and Japan alone accounting for nearly 92 per cent. The alliances between the triad and the newly industrializing countries account for 2.3 per cent of the alliances, and enterprises from all other developing countries share only 1.5 per cent. Furthermore, the share of the developing countries in alliances in biotechnology, new materials, and information technology is a fraction of 1 per cent. Finally, a much smaller proportion of the strategic technology alliances entered into by the developing country enterprises concerns the core technologies. Table 2.4 shows that, whereas the share of core technologies in strategic alliances within the developed economies was 73 per cent, only 23 per cent of those entered into by the developing country enterprises were in core technologies.

In the case of industrial automation technology, Alcorta (1995) has observed that large internationalized oligopolies, with a few exceptions based in developed countries, are taking a pivotal role in the industry's fate, either by increasing their market share or, indirectly, through their control of key steps in the productive chain, and developing country firms are increasingly relegated to the rank of minor partners. Kumar (1995b) attributed the declining importance of arm's length licensing and minority foreign owned

Table 2.3 International distribution of strategic technology alliances, 1980–9

Fields of technology	Number of alliances	% for developed economies	% for triad*	% for triad-NICs	% for triad-LCDs	Other
Biotechnology	846	99.1	94.1	0.4	0.1	0.5
New materials	430	96.5	93.5	2.3	1.2	–
Computer	199	98.0	96.0	1.5	0.5	–
Industrial automation	281	96.1	95.0	2.1	1.8	–
Microelectronics	387	95.9	95.1	3.6	–	0.5
Software	346	99.1	96.2	0.6	0.3	–
Telecom.	368	97.5	92.1	1.6	0.3	0.5
Misc. info. tech.	148	93.3	92.6	5.4	0.7	0.7
Automation	205	84.9	82.9	9.8	5.4	–
Aviation	228	96.9	94.3	0.9	1.3	0.9
Chemical	410	87.6	80.0	3.9	7.1	1.5
Food and beverages	42	90.5	76.2	9.5	–	–
Heavy electricals	141	96.5	92.2	1.4	2.1	–
Machine tools/ instruments	95	100.0	100.0	–	–	–
Others	66	90.9	77.3	1.5	4.5	3.0
Total	4192	95.7	91.9	2.3	1.5	0.5

* USA, Japan and Europe
Source: Freeman and Hagedoorn (1992)

joint ventures as means of technology transfers to the closely held nature of the new technologies and the relative reluctance of their owners to transfer them unaccompanied by ownership and control. Because of their pervasive applications in a wide range of sectors, these technologies are seen by their owners as key instruments of technological competitiveness. This has prompted a wave of technological protectionism in the industrialized countries which includes their attempts to establish new, strengthened rules for the protection of intellectual property world-wide and the promotion of national capabilities in these core technologies by a variety of policy instruments, as described later in this chapter. All these trends tend to raise barriers to entry for newcomers in these technologies.

TECHNONATIONALISM AND TECHNOLOGICAL PROTECTIONISM IN INDUSTRIALIZED COUNTRIES

Growing internationalization of markets over the past years has emphasized the role of technology as a key element of international competitiveness. Hence, technologies are not available any more on an off-the-shelf basis at relatively low prices as in the 1970s, as technology suppliers are apprehensive of creating their own competitors. This explains the relative slow-down of technology transfers to developing countries in recent years (Dahlman *et al.* i, 1995: 176–7).

In order to retain and further sharpen the technological edge of their corporate enterprises, governments of industrialized countries have been supporting the technological activities of national enterprises through a wide variety of government–industry complexes. The governments of Japan, the US and major EU member states such as Germany, France, the UK and the Netherlands have already taken steps to strengthen the technological competitiveness of national enterprises through increasing subsidization of research in a manner that could be termed as a 'technology race' (Roobeek, 1990). The focus of the extensive subsidies provided by the governments to their enterprises is on the core technologies, viz., microelectronics and information technology, biotechnology and new materials (see Roobeek, 1990,

Table 2.4 Shares of core technologies in strategic technology alliances and technology transfer agreements, 1980–9

Region	Share of core technologies in strategic technology alliances, %	Share of core technologies in technology transfer agreements, %
Triad	73.5	61.4
Developed economies	73.0	60.9
Triad-NICs	53.6	52.4
Triad-LDCs	23.4	38.5

Source: Freeman and Hagedoorn (1992)

Chapter 4, for a detailed account). Table 2.5 shows that the governments in France, Germany, the UK and the US, for instance, accounted for 48.8, 37, 34.2 and 47 per cent of total gross R&D expenditure in their respective countries. The figures summarized in Table 2.6 show an increasing proportion of GNP spent on R&D in the industrialized countries as a result of encouragement provided by their governments. Furthermore, nearly 20, 11, 15 and 28 per cent respectively of R&D performed by business enterprises was directly funded by the governments. The government subsidization of R&D activity is widely perceived to be a part of strategic trade policy in the industrialized countries, designed to enhance their national enterprises' competitive edge (see Scherer and Belous, 1994: 35).

Complementing the national programmes of collaborative research, the EU established a number of Community-wide technology development programmes in the 1980s known as framework programmes. The European Framework Programmes have brought together European industries, universities and research centres in joint initiatives in the form of transnational projects since 1984. The EU contributes one half of the cost of the projects, the other half being borne by the participating firms. The first framework programme (1984–7) had a total budget of ECU 3.7 billion; the second (1987–91), a budget of ECU 5.4 billion; and the third Framework Programme (1990–4) tying up with the second programme will have a budget of ECU 7.7 billion (see Kumar, 1992a, for details). The major focus of these programmes is on strengthening the EU's competitiveness in new and emerging technologies such as microelectronics and information technology, biotechnology, and advanced materials, in view of the widespread linkages these core technologies have with other sectors of the economy. Almost all the subsidies go to the private enterprises that undertake R&D projects or participate in the joint projects undertaken with other EU enterprises for eventual commercialization of the technologies developed. This phenomenon contributes to increasing privatization of new knowledge in these core technologies. In the US and Japan much of the knowledge in these core technologies is already in the private domain. A further concentration of scientific knowledge in these areas in the private sector has

Table 2.5 Patterns of R&D financing in select industrialized countries, 1992

	Government's share of total R&D expenditure, %	Direct government's share of R&D performed by business enterprises, %
France	48.8*	19.8†
Germany	37.0	10.7
United Kingdom	34.2*	14.6
United States	47.0	28.3

* belongs to 1991; † belongs to 1990
Source: compiled from OECD (1993): Table 1 for the respective countries

Table 2.6 R&D expenditure as a percentage of gross national product, 1980–93

Region/country	1980	1985	1990	1993
World	1.85	2.22	2.55	n.a.
Developing countries	0.52	0.54	0.64	n.a.
Africa	0.28	0.25	0.25	n.a.
Asia*	1.40	1.77	2.05	n.a.
India	0.63	0.74	0.89	0.83
China	1.50	1.00	0.80	0.63
Latin America and Caribbean	0.44	0.43	0.40	0.40
Arab states	0.97	0.94	0.76	0.40
Developed countries	2.22	2.62	2.92	n.a.
Europe	1.81	2.02	2.21	n.a.
North America	2.23	2.66	3.16	n.a.

* including Japan
Source: UNESCO *Statistical Year Book 1994*: Table 5.1; Gu (1995) for China; UNESCO *World Science Report 1996*

serious implications for the access of developing countries as well as for research priorities. A high degree of privatization of research in the area of biotechnology in the US, for instance, has stunted dissemination of even basic scientific information on advances which used to be available to scientists through professional channels such as conference presentations and publications in learned journals. Furthermore, with privatization, the research priorities are dictated more by commercial prospects than long-term considerations of sustainability.

NEW INTERNATIONAL REGIME FOR INTELLECTUAL PROPERTY PROTECTION

The international environment with respect to intellectual property has changed considerably with the conclusion of the Uruguay Round of Multilateral Trade Negotiations. The TRIPs agreement accommodates the demands of the industrialized countries for higher international standards of protection by mandating the extension of patentability to virtually all fields of technology recognized in developed country patent systems, by prolonging the patent protection for a uniform term of twenty years, and by providing legal recognition of the patentee's exclusive rights to import the patented products. The patent rights are enjoyable without discrimination as to the place of invention, the field of technology and whether products are imported or locally produced. All the signatories to the trade negotiations, therefore, are obliged to harmonize their intellectual property regimes and to provide product patents for pharmaceuticals and chemicals. The coverage of the patent protection has also been expanded by the provision for patents on micro-organisms and protection of plant varieties either by patents or by an effective *sui generis* system, or by any combination thereof. An implication of the inclusion of intellectual property protection within the purview of the World Trading Organization is the possibility of retaliation against countries not complying with the TRIPs obligations by amending their national patents legislation. The retaliation against developing countries could include withdrawal of GSP benefits.

This development has considerable implications for the process of acquisition of local technological capability by developing countries. The provision of product patents on chemical and pharmaceutical products, for instance, would adversely affect the process of innovative activity of the developing country enterprises in the manufacture of chemicals covered by patents. The development of new chemical compounds is generally beyond the capability of most developing country enterprises in view of the huge resources involved. Therefore they focus attention on process innovations for the known chemicals and bulk drugs. This activity has been an important source of learning in developing countries. Indeed, most industrialized countries encouraged local learning through soft patent laws and the absence of product patents in chemicals in the early stages of their development. Japan did not provide for product patents until as late as 1977 and South Korea until the late 1980s. Furthermore, the recognition of importing as working of patent may erode the ability of developing countries to license technologies and set up manufacturing units unless the patent holders, very often large MNEs, are willing to start local production. Finally, the extension of intellectual property protection to plant varieties would increase the outgo of royalties for the breeder lines of the seed companies, while the basic raw material for the development of these varieties, i.e. the genetic diversity which is largely found in developing countries and is supposedly the work of generations of farmers in these countries, is generally available to them free.

EMERGING REGIME ON INTERNATIONAL INVESTMENTS AND TRANSFER OF TECHNOLOGY

To restructure the international technological relations and for the redressal of potential misuse of monopoly power, certain initiatives had been initiated by the international community in the 1970s through the establishment of an International Code of Conduct on Technology Transfer, and a United Nations Code of Conduct for Transnational Corporations. However, negotiations in both cases have proved to be cumbersome because of the rigid attitude adopted by the industrialized countries. The negotiations on the International Code of Conduct on Technology Transfer, for instance, are yet to be completed despite convening six sessions of the UN Conference between 1979 and 1985. Further, the efficacy of the Code, if it ever comes into being, is open to question, as it has now been reduced to a mere set of 'universally acceptable recommendations' rather than a legally binding instrument. The Code will not apply to transactions between a resident but foreign-owned and/or controlled entity and local ones, nor will the restrictions be imposed on intra-firm transactions by MNEs. Similarly, the United Nations Commission on TNCs undertook the preparation of an international code on foreign direct investment way back in 1976. The Commission had forwarded a draft of the code agreed upon after protracted negotiations in 1991 to the Economic and Social Council and then to the General Assembly for action. However, the code was abandoned because of the lack of a consensus, as the Western countries felt that it did 'not provide enough safeguards for investors' (United Nations, *Transnationals*, 4(3)). In fact the intergovernmental group convened by the UN General Assembly in 1992 to finalize the code recommended finding alternative methods to encourage global FDIs and strengthen the investor–host country relationships, as no consensus was possible on the draft code.

While the initiatives that were meant to protect the interests of host countries have been blocked or abandoned, those protecting investors and their interests have been launched over the past decade and have been successful, as these had the backing of the industrialized countries that are the sources of almost all FDI outflows. These include an Agreement on Trade Related Investment Measures (TRIMs) included in the Uruguay Round, and recent negotiations launched by the OECD countries for a multilateral investment treaty. The TRIMs agreement obliges the developing member countries of the World Trade Organization to phase out all trade related performance requirements imposed on enterprises, such as local content regulations and export obligations within a period of five years. Recently, the EU, the US and Japan launched renewed efforts to establish a multilaterally negotiated regime for foreign investment not limited to trade related investments that are covered by the TRIMs agreement of the WTO. The objectives of these initiatives, among others, are to establish right of entry, rules prohibiting favourable treatment of national over foreign firms, ownership restrictions and profit repatriation. These initiatives tend to diminish the ability of developing country governments to direct FDI inflows according to their developmental goals.

STRUCTURAL ADJUSTMENT AND TECHNOLOGICAL CAPABILITY IN DEVELOPING COUNTRIES

Over the past fifteen years a large number of developing countries have undertaken the liberalization of the trade and investment regimes in their economies as a part of structural adjustment programmes. These reforms have tended to make these economies much more open than before. The recently concluded multilateral trade negotiations place further obligations on developing countries with respect to the liberalization of trade, and on their policy regimes with respect to intellectual property rights, FDI, and trade in services. Developing countries have committed to expand tariff bindings – commitments that tariffs will not exceed particular bound levels – to cover 61 per cent of their imports compared to 13 per cent earlier. They have also offered $15 billion worth of concessions by way of reducing their trade-weighted average bound tariff on imports from industrialized countries by 28 per cent (World Bank, 1995). This means that developing country enterprises can no longer enjoy protected domestic markets. They have to be internationally competitive even to retain their domestic markets.

The other implication of the structural adjustment programmes is with respect to their possible adverse impact on local technological effort within the economies. An important aspect of the adjustment relates to the elimination of budget deficits of governments. In developing countries, the scope of additional revenue generation is normally limited specially along with reduction in tariff rates. Therefore, some heads of government expenditure are reduced. As scientific and technological activities do not affect the economy in the short run, they are generally one of those to be affected adversely. One may argue that the increased role that is assigned to the private sector with the structural adjustment programmes may lead to the private sector more than offsetting any reduction in public funded R&D expenditure. This, however, may not happen automatically because R&D is known to be a highly uncertain activity with high externalities. The private entrepreneurs undertaking it are unable to extract all the benefits from it. Therefore, it is generally not taken up without an active intervention and support by the government. Indeed, industrialized country governments are known to encourage the R&D activity of their national champions to strengthen their international competitiveness by subsidization.

Yet another factor in structural adjustment which may be affecting the R&D activity of local enterprises adversely could be the liberalization of technology import and FDI policies that generally accompany it. In view of the several commercial attractions of imported technology and its trustworthiness, local generation of technology which is inherently risky will not be taken up in the absence of any protection to it from foreign technologies, as we have argued elsewhere (Kumar, 1990c).

The trends on the significance of R&D expenditure in national income in the world summarized in Table 2.6 tend to substantiate the proposition that structural adjustment has led to declining outlays on R&D. It is apparent that, in the regions that underwent structural adjustment in the 1980s, i.e. Africa, Latin America and the Caribbean, the proportion of national resources devoted to R&D had declined by 1990. Asia is the only continent where it has gone up, but this is due to the rapidly expanding R&D activity in Japan, South Korea, Taiwan and Singapore. In countries like India and China, which undertook adjustment and reforms, the proportion of R&D has declined.

Enos (1995) found in the case of four Sub-Saharan economies, Ghana,

Kenya, Tanzania and Uganda, that the total expenditures in the pursuit of science and technology increased substantially after these countries embarked upon structural adjustment programmes, but this increase came about chiefly as a result of the substantial increase in the foreign funding of these activities. This trend was accompanied by the shifting of the locus of decision-making away from these countries to donor countries, and research priorities were determined by the donor's, rather than local, interests.

The neglect of domestic R&D activities in developing countries will have serious repercussions on their local capabilities and will affect not only their ability to absorb and adapt the fruits of technological developments elsewhere in the world but even their ability to make the right technological choices and obtain favourable terms in technology transfer contracts. It would, therefore, constrain their ability technologically to upgrade their manufactured product profile and could undermine their international competitiveness in both the medium and the long run.

CONCLUDING REMARKS AND POLICY IMPLICATIONS

The trends reviewed in this chapter suggest that the possibilities to build up local capabilities behind protectionist barriers are much more limited now than earlier. So are the possibilities of absorbing the spillovers from technological advances taking place elsewhere with softer intellectual property protection and protection to local enterprises, as most industrialized and newly industrializing economies could in the early stages of their development. The emergence of new core technologies further complicates the prospects of capability building because of their special characteristics. These technologies are characterized by very high skill intensity, a rapidly moving technological frontier not allowing standardization and hence catching up, increasing privatization of basic research, thus choking their diffusion through professional channels. These technologies are increasingly coming into the hold of large corporations in the industrialized countries through cross-licensing, strategic alliances and joint venture formations. There are indications that developing countries are being marginalized by the new technological revolution. In view of the fact that these technologies find applications in a very wide spectrum of economic activities, the inability of developing countries to build capability in these technologies may have serious implications for their international competitiveness. This would tend to point towards the urgency of a response by the governments of these countries to step up their efforts to build up capabilities. Government intervention in the industrialized world in the area of technologies, especially new technologies, is substantial and takes the form of R&D in the public-funded laboratories as well as encouragement of R&D in enterprises by R&D subsidization, formation of research consortia, protection of national champions by preferences in public procurement, etc. Ironically, at a time when developing countries need to step up their technological efforts more than ever to at least try to absorb and harness the vast potential of new technologies for their development, the scale and extent of technological activity appears to have gone down in recent years. This is because of the compulsions of balancing budgets under structural adjustment programmes which have led to declining public funding of these activities and have not been matched by an increasing private sector initiative.

This development is to be noted with concern as it will have serious consequences on their international competitiveness. The viability and relevance of government intervention in building capability specifically in new technologies is demonstrated in the next chapter with an illustration from biotechnology in a number of developing countries where governments did manage to put an institutional infrastructure in place for building some capability, and to harness its potential for solving some of their specific problems such as improving the productivity levels in their important export commodities. International institutional cooperation has also supplemented the government initiatives in a useful manner. The other core technologies have not received that kind of policy response from either international organizations or governments in developing countries. These are seemingly also less open than biotechnology in terms of building capability, hence demanding perhaps even a greater level of government promotion and support. The nature of governmental intervention has to be defined in accordance with the characteristics of these core technologies, taking note of the changed organizational setting where private enterprises assume a greater role in the economic activity of countries. The conventional approaches of limiting government funding to the state-owned laboratories may not be appropriate, especially in view of the difficulties such laboratories may face in orienting themselves to the needs of enterprises and commercialization and diffusion of their research. Government initiative would be most critical in creating an institutional infrastructure that could catalyse the process of capability building by providing support to enterprises in their own technological effort. Furthermore, governments will have to find resources to subsidize the corporate technological efforts at least in the early phases. In view of the substantial externalities of technological activities, even industrialized country governments contribute directly to the R&D spending of their enterprises, as reviewed above. Some countries have promoted technological activities of enterprises with subsidized credit. Kim (1993) has shown that 94 per cent of the South Korean corporate R&D in 1987 was financed through 'preferential loans', granted at low interest rates from state-controlled banks and public funds. The Korean government has also supported the technological effort of local enterprises in other ways, such as tax exemptions, tax credits for expenditures on human capital upgrading for research, accelerated depreciation on R&D investments, import duty concessions, establishment of industry research institutes, and

31

excise concessions on technology-intensive products (Lall, 1995). The provision of risk capital for new technology-based ventures may be another instrument for promoting the creation of capability in new technologies in developing countries. In that context it may be recalled that the venture capital industry has been instrumental in funding new technology enterprises in the US which spearheaded the technological developments in these areas.

To conclude, therefore, government intervention is crucial for technological capability building in developing countries. The form that governmental intervention takes would vary from case to case (see Lall, 1995, for a rationale of government intervention for building technological and industrial capability in developing countries and the different forms it has taken in select countries). It may differ for different branches of technologies and also according to the stage of development of the country and the extent of maturity of the business enterprises undertaking the technological effort.

3

NEW TECHNOLOGIES AND DEVELOPING COUNTRIES
A case study of capability building in biotechnology

INTRODUCTION

Recent advances in biotechnology research comprise techniques which enable the manipulation of the inherited characteristics of living organisms and plants through several asexual means. As indicated in Chapter 2, the application of these techniques could affect production processes in such diverse areas as agriculture, food processing, energy, chemicals, health and medicine in a fundamental way. The biotechnology revolution, as it has come to be known, has important implications for the developing world. These technologies have tremendous development potential and can prove to be valuable allies of developing countries in their struggle against poverty, hunger and disease, and in their effort to become more self-reliant economies. The emerging trends in the global biotechnology industry suggest that research and production in the area are geared more by commercial rather than development potential of these technologies. This poses a major challenge for the developing country governments as well as international development organizations.

This chapter begins by briefly discussing the potential of biotechnologies for fostering a sustainable pattern of development in developing countries. The following section summarizes the main emerging trends taking place in the global biotechnology industry and their implications for the access of developing countries to the new technologies. The chapter then goes on to discuss the imperatives of building local capability in a developing country and examines the issues involved. It reviews the experiences of a few developing countries that embarked on biotechnology capability building. It also discusses the role of international cooperation in the area. Conclusions are drawn in the final section.

BIOTECHNOLOGIES AND SUSTAINABLE DEVELOPMENT IN DEVELOPING COUNTRIES

Biotechnologies can prove to be instrumental in solving a number of pressing problems of developing countries, such as hunger, poverty and disease. In what follows, we summarize the potential of these technologies for sustainable development in developing countries (see Kumar, 1993, for more details and further sources).

Food security

By the turn of the century the world's population will have risen to over six billion. Merely to maintain the current consumption levels, an increase of 26 per cent in the world's average grains yields will be needed. The bulk of this increase will be required in the developing countries. Unlike in the past, when yield increases were achieved under favourable cropping conditions by the Green Revolution, future improvements in yields must come from the productivity improvement of traditional farmers cultivating low-yield crops under marginal conditions and with little dependence on purchased inputs. Integrated with conventional plant breeding, biotechnologies can play an important role in providing the basis for the economic and ecological sustainability of further increases in agricultural yield and thus ensure food security for developing countries. Some illustrations in this context are as follows:

- Biotechnology can help improve agricultural productivity by raising the ceiling of yields through enhancement of the efficiency of photosynthesis. It can also help in bridging the gap between actual and potential yields by accelerating the pace of plant breeding. Tissue culture techniques, for instance, can be used for the rapid multiplication of single superior virus-free and disease-free (elite) plants and the regeneration of plants difficult to propagate sexually. Phenomenal gains in yield have already been reported in different parts of the world through the application of tissue culture in oil palm, coconut, banana, tubers, and other plants. Techniques like embryo rescue, protoplast fusion, and the use of DNA vectors, enable plant breeders to overcome the barriers of sexual incompatibility in transferring desirable traits.
- Biotechnology can assume a crucial role in the reclamation of poor soils and wastelands. For instance, in South Asia and Southeast Asia alone about 86.5 million hectares of land can be made productive with rice varieties tolerant to salinity and alkalinity. In India, biotechnology is being used to develop mustard plants tolerant to salinity as part of a technology mission aiming to achieve self-sufficiency in edible oils. Similarly, adaptation of cereal crops to drought-prone areas could be valuable for solving the food problem in Sub-Saharan Africa.

- Biotechnology can accelerate the development of low-input agriculture. This will be of special significance for developing countries with large populations of small and marginal farmers. Low-input agriculture requires disease-resistant and pest-resistant varieties with an ability to fix nitrogen. Biological nitrogen fixation through various agents, such as blue-green algae that are symbiotic with the water fern Azola and rhizobia in symbiosis with legumes, offers a great potential for increasing the agricultural yield in developing countries without increasing their dependence on chemical fertilizers.
- Biotechnology can also be used to redress the imbalances caused by the Green Revolution. The Green Revolution covered only a small band of cereals and did not benefit a wide range of crops produced and consumed by the world's poor, such as cassava, yams, and sweet potatoes, which are vegetatively propagated. Biotechnology not only has a tremendous potential for improving the productivity of these crops but can also be applied to raise their nutritive value.
- Biotechnological techniques provide the basis for the ecological sustainability of high yields by reducing risks from pests, pathogens, and weeds and promoting conservation of genetic resources. The genetic material in the wild species contributes billions of dollars yearly to the world economy through high yields and by saving crops from diseases, and through new drugs and medicines. These are crucial resources for ensuring the sustainability of long-term food security. The new techniques allow preservation of cloned DNA and materials having DNA in their native state for genetic conservation. Further, somaclonal variation presents opportunities for adding to the pool of genetic variability.
- The potential spectrum of biological pesticides occurring naturally or in the form of genetically restructured organisms that are specifically pathogenic to important pests, parasites, or weeds is enormous and remains largely unexplored. Integrated pest management which reduces the need for agrochemicals through the use of natural pesticides and integrated cropping patterns is especially appropriate for small and marginal farmers in developing countries.

Resource saving in industry

A great variety of food processing, and chemical processes such as fermentation, involve the use of microbes. The efficiency of these processes and the nutritive value of the product can be increased through the selection of more productive microbial strains, control of culture conditions, and through adaptation of the fermentation processes. These techniques can be employed not only for the treatment of effluents, but also for the production of valuable products from industrial wastes. Thus, these technologies can help in solving pollution problems while also generating additional added value. For instance, single cell proteins can be produced from molasses, paper mill effluents, or hydrocarbons, and can be used as high-protein cattle feeds.

More efficient exploitation of mineral resources

Metals can be extracted from low-grade ores with biotechnological techniques. Thus, modified bacteria can be used to accelerate the production of chemical solutions that wash out normally insoluble mineral compounds containing such metals as copper, zinc, nickel and lead. Bacterial leaching can be used to extract the remaining minerals from mining and metallurgical wastes. It can also help in extracting the remaining oil from dead oil wells.

Rural industrialization

With biotechnological advances, it is possible to integrate agriculture with the production of food, animal feeds, energy, fertilizer, and a number of industrial products. Such integrated systems can help to generate valuable resources from agricultural wastes and to foster decentralized rural industrialization in developing countries. The recycling of wastes into energy helps reduce the pressure on conventional sources of energy. Certain encouraging experiences from Brazil, China and India with these food-energy integrated systems are now available and could be extended to other developing countries.

Population and health

Population explosion is a major developmental problem in most developing countries. Biotechnologies can be of great help in the efforts of these countries to reduce the birth rate. Biotechnological techniques are being employed in India to develop infertility vaccines and better and more effective kits for early detection of pregnancy. In the areas of health and medicine, biotechnologies have led to the development of new drugs (e.g. TPA, a vital life-saving medicine for heart attack) and to the production of more efficient substitutes of known drugs (e.g. humulin, human insulin). These techniques also have a tremendous potential in immuno-diagnostics and the development of vaccines.

Reforestation and control of pollution

Some of the biotechnological techniques, such as tissue culture, are invaluable for programmes of reforestation and social forestry. They enable the rapid regeneration of tree saplings and the faster growth of trees. They can also improve fibre quality, disease resistance, and growth under adverse physical conditions. Further, these techniques provide more efficient means of fighting the menace of urban and industrial pollution. With them, detoxification of almost any substance is conceivable. One of the first modified micro-organisms to be patented was actually a bacterium capable of 'eating' oil spills.

Balance of payments and international competitiveness

Most of the developing countries suffer from a perpetual balance of payments crisis. Another aspect of sustainability for them is the potential of conserving and earning foreign exchange resources. Through the development of crops requiring lower inputs of chemical fertilizers, pesticides and herbicides, by contributing to the self-sufficiency of food, and by generating energy and chemicals from the recycling of biomass and other wastes, biotechnologies can help developing countries to save scarce foreign exchange resources. Similarly, biotechnology applications can contribute to the improvement of international competitiveness of many primary and industrial products of developing countries. As indicated earlier, biotechnology applications can increase the productivity and hence the competitiveness of many export-oriented crops and industries in developing countries. Tissue culture, for instance, is being extensively used in different parts of the developing world to improve the productivity of important export crops such as oil palm (in Malaysia and Costa Rica), coconut (India), cardamom (India), banana (Colombia and India) and tea (India and Sri Lanka). Bacterial leaching can similarly improve the competitiveness of mining industries which are often export-oriented. The efficiency and productivity of a number of food and other agroprocessing industries using microbial fermentation could also be improved with biotechnology applications. Therefore, biotechnologies can potentially contribute a great deal to a more balanced trade in developing countries.

Thus the developmental potential of biotechnologies appears to be tremendous. Given the proper policy framework for their development and exploitation they can provide to the developing countries valuable means to expedite the process of their development and pursue a pattern of growth with positive income distribution effects. This potential, however, remains unexploited because of the lack of local capability in developing countries and the emerging structure of biotechnology industries that is driven more by commercial prospects than development potential, as will be seen later.

EMERGING BIOTECHNOLOGY INDUSTRY

The bulk of biotechnology R&D is concentrated in the industrialized countries – the US, Japan and Europe. The emerging biotechnology industry in these countries is characterized by a high degree of privatization of knowledge and domination by large multinational enterprises, vertical integration, and proprietary ownership, as summarized below.

Private control and concentration of knowledge

Research in biotechnology was spearheaded by small specialist firms floated by professional scientists and supported by venture capital firms. Gradually, MNEs, especially those with primary interests in pharmaceutical, chemical, food, and energy industries, recognized the potential of biotechnology for their businesses. Besides setting up their own R&D programmes, these MNEs have established strong links with specialist biotech firms through takeovers and acquisitions, as shown in Table 3.1. Besides actual takeovers and acquisitions, large MNEs have entered into a variety of joint ventures, contractual agreements and strategic alliances, giving them exclusive marketing rights over the fruits of research, as shown in Table 3.2.

MNEs have also contracted much of the biotechnology research carried out in the universities and public-funded research institutions, and thus enjoy the right of prior access and patent ownership. For instance, DuPont took exclusive proprietary rights over the 'gene gun', a particle accelerator and a valuable tool for genetic engineering developed by Cornell University scientists in 1989. In the USA, for instance, nearly half of the companies engaged in biotechnology research have arrangements with universities. One-fourth of all biotechnology research in US universities in the mid-1980s was supported by the industry (Dembo *et al.*, 1989). Table 3.3 provides some illustrations of the trend of the increasing commercial character of research conducted in the universities and public funded research organizations. The concentration of knowledge in a few corporations has increased with the recent mega-mergers in industry, e.g. Glaxo and Wellcome, Pharmacia and Upjohn, and Sandoz and Ciba. Among the major and explicit motivations for these mergers has been the intention to exploit synergies in competences and scale economies in R&D effort. An immediate consequence of this trend

Table 3.1 Select acquisitions of specialist biotechnology companies by large MNEs

Biotech company	Year	Taken over by
Biogen	1980	Monsanto
Collagen	1980	Monsanto
Cytogen	1983	Lederle
BioVec	1984	Mitsubishi
Genetics Systems	1985	Bristol Myers
Agrigenetics	1985	Lubrizol
Hybritech	1986	Eli Lilly
Genetech	1990	Roche
Genetics Institute	1991	American Home Products
Systemix	1991	Sandoz
Applied Immune Sciences	1993	Rhone-Poulenc Rorer
Affymax	1995	Glaxo Wellcome
Genetic Therapy	1995	Sandoz

Source: Ernst and Young, *Biotech Industry Annual Reports* (various years)

of private control of knowledge is that there is little flow of basic scientific information through the traditional scientific channels, such as publication in learned journals, conferences, and other professional interactions.

Furthermore, as was shown in Chapter 2, Western governments are supporting the monopoly position of their enterprises in core technologies to maintain their country's competitive edge. Biotechnologies happen to be among the technologies that have received substantial government subsidies and research funding. The European Union, for instance, has launched a number of framework programmes to promote the capability building of European

Table 3.2 Select instances of R&D arrangements between biotech companies and MNEs

Biotech company	MNE	Type of arrangement	Product/area
Centocor	Hoffman LaRoche	joint venture	monoclonal antibodies
Centocor	FMC Corp.	joint venture	immuno-diagnostics
Biotechnica International	Seagram	strategic alliance	
Biotechnica International	Uniroyal	research contract	biological nitrogen fixation
DNA Plant Technology	Campbell Soup	research contract	high-solid tomato
Intellicorp	Amoco Corp	joint venture	biotech software
Nova Pharma.	Celanese Corp.	joint venture	drug delivery system
Calgene	Rhone-Poulenc	research contract	herbicide-tolerant sunflower
Cetus	Kodak	joint development	human diagnostics
Immunex	Kodak	joint venture	immunology
Amgen	Johnson & Johnson	joint development	hepatitis vaccine
Amgen	SmithKline Beecham	strategic alliance	porcine somatoprine
Chinon Corp.	Ciba-Geigy	joint venture	vaccines
DNA Plant Technology	DuPont	research contract	plant varieties
Calgene	Ciba-Geigy	research contract	disease-resistant crops
Endotronics	Celanese	strategic alliance	immunotherapy
Calgene	Nestlé	joint development	herbicide-tolerant soyabeans
PDT	Pharmacia	exclusive licensing	photodynamic cancer therapy
Sequana Therapeutics	Boehringer Ingelheim	research collaboration	asthma drugs
Biocompatibles International	Johnson & Johnson	joint venture	drug delivery stents
Oxford Asymmetry	Pfizer	joint venture	combinatorial chemistry
British Biotech	Glaxo Wellcome	exclusive licensing	arthritis drug

Source: adapted from Dembo, Dias and Morehouse (1989): pp. 48–51; and Ernst and Young, *Biotechnology Industry Annual Reports* (various years)

enterprises in the area of biotechnology and hence their competitiveness. These programmes include the Biotechnology Action Programme (BAP), European Collaborative Linkage of Agriculture and Industry through Research (ECLAIR), Food-linked Agro-Industrial Research (FLAIR), and Biotechnology Research for Innovation Development and Growth in Europe (BRIDGE) (see, among others, Kumar, 1992a, for more details).

Table 3.3 Illustrative university/industry R&D contracts

University	Industry	Product /area
USA		
Rockefeller	Monsanto	photosynthesis research
Washington	Monsanto	hybridomas
Harvard	Monsanto	oligosaccharides
Illinois	Standard Oil of Ohio	crop molecular genetics and genetic engineering
Washington	Monsanto	human diseases and fundamental research
Cornell	Union Carbide, Corning, Kodak	biotechnology institute
MIT	W. R. Grace	micro-organisms
Columbia	Bristol-Myers	gene cloning and rDNA technology
Harvard	DuPont	research grant
Yale	Celanese	enzymes
Washington	Mallinckrodt	hybridoma research
UK		
Oxford	Monsanto	oligosaccharides
Bristol, Birbeck College, Oxford, Leeds, York, Imperial College	Celltech, Glaxo, ICI, RTZ Chemicals	research consortia on protein engineering
Leicester	John Brown Engineers, Dalgety-Spillers, Gallaghers and Whitbread	biotechnology research
France		
Compiegne	Elf Aquitaine	enzyme engineering
Germany		
Heidelberg	BASF	biotechnology research
Cologne, Max Planck Institute	Bayer	biotechnology research
Munich, Max Planck Institute	Hoechst	collaborative project

Source: adapted from Dembo, Dias and Morehouse (1989): pp. 43–7

Vertical integration

The secrecy surrounding biotechnology research has led to a trend of vertical integration among the biotechnology user industries and technology producers. In the area of agrobusiness, the integration has taken the form of major agrochemical corporations taking over the seed businesses on the one hand and biotechnology specialists on the other. This is because the future demand of agrochemicals would depend largely on the type of seeds sold in view of the possibility of manipulation of their characteristics with biotechnology. Table 3.4 shows that agrochemical corporations such as Sandoz, Upjohn, ICI and Dekalb/Pfizer find a place among the top ten seed companies. This trend of integration accelerated especially in the 1980s after the potential of biotechnology to affect agrochemical sales was recognized, as seen from the illustration of ICI shown in Table 3.5. In the second round of vertical integration, food processing companies took over biotechnology companies to benefit from the applications of biotechnologies in their processes. Now it is the turn of the pharmaceutical industry. Ernst & Young's (1994) annual report on biotechnology describes the integration taking place in the biotechnology industry as 'virtual' integration, whereby companies advance or enhance their vertical integration within their value chain without increasing their mass. Within the biotechnology industry, it is most fully visible in the healthcare segment. By aligning between and within their sectors, pharmaceutical and biotechnology companies are equipping themselves to pursue their long-term goals within a global market place.

Proprietary ownership

Another marked trend in the area of biotechnology is the one of increasing proprietary ownership of biotechnology-based processes and products

Table 3.4 Seed sales of world's largest seed companies

Company	1990 seed sales US$ million
Pioneer	840
Sandoz/Hilleshog	473
Limagrain	335
Upjohn	270
ICI	250
Cargill	240
Dekalb/Pfizer	205
Takii	157
KWS	153
Sakata	153

Source: Walsh *et al.* (1991): Table 21

Table 3.5 Acquisitions by ICI Seeds

Year	Company
1985	Garst Seed Company
1986	Sinclair McGill
1987	SES
1987	Miln Marsters
1987	Rohm and Haas
	(Garnetocide technology)
1989	Contiseeds
1990	Agroplant
1990	Super Crost

Source: Walsh *et al.* (1991): Table 23

through the use of industrial patent laws and plant breeders' rights to maintain a monopoly position. Historically, living organisms have not been subject to patent protection. There has been an increasing tendency in the industrialized countries in recent years to provide patent protection to biotechnology-based innovations through modifications of laws. In 1980, the US Supreme Court allowed patenting of a modified micro-organism. In 1986, a plant variety was granted a utility patent like an industrial innovation in the US, which so far had been covered only by plant breeders' rights. In 1987, the US Patent Office announced the industrial patenting of higher life forms, including pets and livestock. A universal application of these patents is being sought through harmonization of the intellectual property regimes of different countries in the framework of the recently concluded multilateral trade negotiations.

Implications of these trends for developing countries

The increasing private and proprietary character of biotechnology research has important implications for the access of developing countries and determination of research priorities.

Access of developing countries to biotechnologies

The growing commercial character of university and public funded research institutions, together with trade secrecy, has made the traditional means of transfer of basic technical information, such as interactions among scientists and publications in learned journals, insignificant. The closely held nature of the technology has made the markets for biotechnology highly imperfect, diminishing the prospects of its transfer to developing countries on reasonable terms and through appropriate channels.

Research priorities

The extreme degree of the private and commercial character of biotechnology research results in the determination of research priorities by commercial prospects and by the global strategies of MNEs. In agribusiness, for instance, given a nearly $16 billion market of herbicides, insecticides and other crop protection products (see Table 3.6), the agrochemical corporations which now control the bulk of the seed industry attached top priority to incorporating herbicide and insecticide resistance in seeds. The herbicides' usage has a potential to displace a large proportion of the labour force currently employed in developing countries to weed out weeds and herbs physically. According to an OECD study the herbicide- and pesticide-tolerant seeds were among the first outcomes of agrobiotechnology (see Table 3.7). Clearly, the potential of biotechnology for developing seeds that require little input of chemicals and that save energy and other valuable resources remains largely unutilized.

Substitution of commodity exports

A significant part of biotechnology research in Western countries is actually aimed at the industrial production of certain high-value plant secondary metabolites, such as flavourings, fragrances and medicinal plants, and other commodities like sugar and gum Arabic, presently imported from developing countries. These developments, like those resulting from other frontier technologies, such as flexible automation systems, new materials, etc., will further diminish the place of developing countries in the international division of labour (Junne, 1988). The development of sweeteners such as high fructose corn syrup and Aspartame has already affected adversely developing countries such as the Philippines that export sugar. The factory production of 'natural' vanillin through cell culture could adversely affect the lives of thousands of vanilla farmers in Madagascar. According to estimates made by Panchamukhi and Kumar (1988), the developing world

Table 3.6 World market for crop protection in the late 1980s (US$ million)

Region	Herbicides	Insecticides	Fungicides	Diverse
North America	3547	1208	364	346
Europe	2333	896	1774	469
Japan, Australia and Southeast Asia	1444	1602	1126	143
Latin America (Brazil, Mexico, Argentina)	640	424	190	31

Source: OECD (1992): Table 26

Table 3.7 Probable evolution of agrobiotechnology

1990–3	Herbicide, pesticide tolerance
1993–6	Processing improvements
1996–9	Industrial pharmaceutical production
1999–2003	Environmental tolerance
2003–6	Direct yield enhancements

Source: OECD (1992): Table 25

could lose about US$10 billion of its annual export earnings from biotechnology-based commodity substitutions in the near future. The loss of export earnings would only aggravate the already precarious condition of developing countries.

Local technological capability and plant breeding

The trend of granting intellectual property rights (IPRs) and their universal recognition has important implications for developing countries. These rights grant exclusive monopoly over the import, manufacturing, and selling of any plant varieties or livestock containing patented traits to companies owning such rights. Even the storing of seeds by farmers for further use out of their output, which is a widespread practice in the developing world, could contravene these monopoly rights. The basic raw materials for genetic manipulation are wild genetic resources which are heavily concentrated in tropical or subtropical areas. These vital resources have been appropriated by the industrialized countries without any compensation (Kloppenberg and Kleinman, 1988). Therefore, granting a monopoly right to a company on a variety for specific traits drawn from genetic resources originating in developing countries amounts to commercial exploitation of those countries' resources by MNEs world-wide without the source countries ever sharing any part of the quasi rent. Besides, IPRs might seriously jeopardize the chances of developing countries to benefit from their own genetic resources for the improvement of their crops with biotechnology, as the MNEs would have already patented much of their genetic material. Much of the *ex situ* genetic resources are already stored in gene banks located in the industrialized countries. Thus, as the South Commission rightly observed, a fatal blow could be dealt to the plant breeding activity in the developing world.

BUILDING LOCAL CAPABILITY IN DEVELOPING COUNTRIES: THE ROLE AND NATURE OF NATIONAL AND INTERNATIONAL INTERVENTION

In the context of the preceding analysis, therefore, the need for developing countries to take initiatives to build an autonomous capability to pursue high priority biotechnology research without any further loss of time cannot be overemphasized. What are the prospects of building capability in a frontier area such as biotechnology in developing countries? There are some who find little prospects of building capability in the area – e.g. according to a European Community report, it would be 'foolish to think that Third World countries with little expertise or resources, can at this stage build a research base in this new technology which can emulate the achievements of the first world' (Thomas, 1993: 2). The report advocates instead promotion of mechanisms to transfer technology.

On the other hand there are others who contend that it is feasible for developing countries to build some workable capability in biotechnology, despite its highly skill-intensive nature. For one thing, unlike other core technologies such as micro-electronics, biotechnology is not highly capital-intensive. Setting up a biotechnology R&D facility calls for relatively modest investments compared to those in other frontier technologies or conventional heavy industries such as steel or petrochemicals. They are relatively open and versatile technologies (e.g. with a lower scientific threshold than other frontier technologies) and are not scale-intensive. Certain skills, capabilities and infrastructure are already available in developing countries, such as those necessary for cloning and tissue culture in plant breeding and certain techniques in molecular biology, which can be upgraded with a little effort. Research costs in developing countries are lower because of lower salaries and wages and low costs of animals. Finally, a rich genetic heritage is an advantage for developing countries (Kumar, 1988).

The biotechnology revolution creates new opportunities for the developing countries for exploiting their traditional advantages in natural resources and low cost labour by combining them with local technological capability. Developing countries have to find entry points in which they can combine existing resources and capabilities with new techniques to strengthen their competitiveness (Weiss, 1992). One possible entry point which a number of countries have adopted is tissue culture, a relatively simple technology which allows developing countries to mobilize cheap labour to augment their plant breeding programmes and to produce disease-free propagation material for edible oil crops such as coconut, oil palm; fruits such as bananas, strawberries; export spices such as cardamom; staple foods such as potato, cassava. The progression from mastering the relatively low-technology tissue culture techniques could be to the development of new varieties of important crops by combining tissue culture with other more advanced breeding methods such as wide crosses by protoplast fusion and anther culture, and eventually to recombinant DNA methods.

Another relatively simple entry point could be improving the efficiency and competitiveness of bio-reactor process industries such as distilleries and beverage manufacture, food processing, organic and amino acids, etc., by using improved imported strains of microbes. They could eventually develop the capability to adapt and modify imported products and develop and produce new products with further selection and genetic modification.

Experiences of developing countries in building local capability in biotechnology

A number of developing countries launched significant national efforts to harness biotechnology for their own economic and social needs during the 1980s. A UNIDO (1991) study examined the policies and programmes of eight of these countries at the end of the 1980s. These were: Brazil, India, China, Mexico, Thailand, Argentina, Cuba and Nigeria. The study concluded that most of these countries had managed to put in place a basic infrastructure for further work in biotechnology and to get started on the necessarily long-term effort of building up their human resources and research facilities in biotechnology. Certainly, these countries are better positioned to try to take advantage of the development potential of biotechnology than those that have made little or no effort thus far. A more recent study by the Intermediary Biotechnology Service (IBS) at ISNAR has evaluated the approach adopted by an overlapping set of ten countries to stimulate biotechnology research in public and private institutions (Komen and Persley, 1993). These countries are: China, Colombia, Egypt, India, Indonesia, Kenya, Malaysia, the Philippines, Thailand, and Zimbabwe. In what follows we summarize the major findings and lessons emerging from these two studies.

The countries studied have broadly followed four approaches to stimulate biotechnology research and create capabilities. Some countries, such as India, China and Thailand, which possess strong capabilities in agricultural research, have preferred to create national coordinating agencies to promote biotechnology development in existing institutions. India, for instance, created the Department of Biotechnology (DBT) within the Ministry of Science and Technology in 1986 to replace the National Biotechnology Board which had been created in 1982. The DBT develops integrated national programmes in biotechnology, supports biotechnology infrastructure development including human resource development, and funds R&D projects at different institutions (Kumar, 1987d). China created the China National Centre for Biotechnology Development (CNCBD) in 1983 as a part of the State Science and Technology Commission. The Centre coordinates all biotechnology R&D activities in research institutes and universities and provides funds for designated areas of applied biotechnology research – in agriculture, health, and protein engineering. Thailand created the National Center for Genetic Engineering and Biotechnology (NCGEB) in 1983 as the main coordination centre for R&D projects in biotechnology. It supports research in the national universities in the areas of tissue culture, plant selection and germplasm conservation, biofertilizers, pest control and rice. It has also supported the setting up of the Bioservice Unit (BSU) as a core facility to provide basic molecular services to researchers at different organizations.

Indonesia and Malaysia, among others, have promoted multiple centres of excellence. The Malaysian government, for instance, provides funding for the Malaysia Agricultural Research and Development Institute (MARDI), the Palm Oil Research Institute of Malaysia (PORIM), the Rubber Research Institute of Malaysia (PRIM) and the Forest Research Institute of Malaysia (FRIM). PORIM, PRIM and FRIM focus on applying tissue culture to their mandated crops. MARDI conducts research on rice, cocoa, vegetables, field crops and ornamentals. MARDI set up a Biotechnology Centre in 1990 to consolidate all its resources related to biotechnology R&D activities. It supports the transfer of the laboratory research results to industry through an Industrial Development Unit. The National Biotechnology Working Group coordinates the activities of these centres of excellence. Indonesia has appointed three agencies to take the lead in facilitating a national network for biotechnology R&D: for agricultural biotechnology, the Agency of Agricultural Research and Development (AARD); for medical biotechnology, the University of Indonesia, Jakarta, and for industrial biotechnology, the Agency for Technology Assessment and Applications (BBPT). In addition, three inter-university centres have been created in agricultural, industrial and medical biotechnology respectively, with the World Bank's assistance. A National Committee for Biotechnology has been set up to formulate policies and programmes for the national development of biotechnology.

The Philippines, Egypt and Cuba, among others, have sought to promote a national biotechnology capability by establishing national research institutes. The Philippines government had set up the National Institute of Biotechnology and Applied Microbiology (BIOTECH) as early as 1979 on the campus of the University of Philippines at Los Banos. BIOTECH's major research thrusts are in nitrogen fixation, biofuel production from agricultural and crop residues, food fermentation, feed production, veterinary antibiotics, plant diagnostics, and plant cell cultures for the production of high value substances. Egypt set up the Agricultural Genetic Research Institute in 1990 with UNDP's assistance. It focuses on the production of virus-free potato mini-tubers through tissue culture and genetic engineering, improvement of rapeseed varieties, and molecular biology and genetic engineering of tomatoes to develop disease-resistant varieties.

Argentina, Brazil, Kenya, Zimbabwe and Colombia, among others, have launched national biotechnology programmes defining priorities and with responsibility for stimulating, coordinating, and facilitating work on biotechnology. In Brazil, Programa Nacional Biotecnologia de Brasil (PRONAB) was created under the National Council of the Development of Science and Technology to integrate and coordinate the diverse institutions and funds involved in biotechnology in the areas of energy, agribreeding and health, with special emphasis on capacity in genetic engineering. Argentina created the National Programme on Biotechnology (PUB) as a part of the Secretariat for Science and Technology. The PUB established priority areas for research and development and grants subsidies for specific biotechnology projects.

These reviews of national efforts in building capabilities in biotechnology in developing countries bring out certain lessons. Very often there is a tendency to pursue the research priorities that are fashionable in the industrialized countries. This leads to efforts which are at best only marginally relevant to the most urgent economic and social needs of the countries concerned. The conversion of research results into marketable products is, as usual, the weakest area in most developing countries. There is little private-sector involvement and foreign direct investment is nearly absent, as opportunities for commercial development are limited. Different countries have taken initiatives for promoting private-sector investment and for commercializing new technologies developed by the public-funded laboratories. In Thailand, for instance, NCGEB and the Department of Biochemistry at Mahidol University have jointly set up a Bioservice Unit to coordinate linkages and transfer novel techniques among government institutions and the private sector. India's DBT has set up the Biotech Consortium India Limited in cooperation with financial institutions for accelerating the process of commercialization of biotechnology in India. BIOTECH in the Philippines has set up pilot plant production of its vaccines and biofertilizers and has entered into marketing arrangements with private-sector enterprises. Once the private entrepreneurs recognize the market potential of the new products, they will be motivated to productionize the technologies. MARDI in Malaysia has a special Industrial Development Unit that supports the transfer of results from laboratory to industry. CNCBD has invested heavily in the Shanghai Centre for Biotechnology Development (SCBD), which will transfer technology and will have capability in further development work involving conversion of basic research into pilot-plant level. The Biotechnology Institute at the National University of Colombia will work with private and public sector industries to promote the transfer of new technology to industry. This experience demonstrates that the commercialization of biotechnology products, like most innovative products, involves substantial development. A case study of the commercialization of the filariasis diagnostic kit in India (Kumar, 1992b) shows that commercialization continues to be the weakest area in indigenous technology development in developing countries. Market uncertainty, the need for further development, upscaling and process engineering may deter local entrepreneurs from coming forward to commercialize the technology. One of the ways to improve this situation is to insist on industry participation (even though its financial contribution may be marginal) in the R&D projects from the start. Adequate provision of venture capital could also be an important means of encouraging industry to undertake potentially risky investments in R&D and commercialize new biotechnology-based products.

International cooperation

While there is no substitute for national effort in building capability in the area of biotechnology, international cooperation has a vital role to play in strengthening biotechnology capability in developing countries. Such cooperation assumes a special significance in view of some trends such as privatization in industrialized countries that make access to significant developments in biotechnology more difficult. Some specific areas in which international cooperation could be of considerable importance include: human resources development; access to basic scientific research and transfer of critical technologies; mobilizing resources for research on the common problems of developing countries; biodiversity conservation; and biosafety.

Some of these concerns have already received attention from the international community. UNIDO has set up an International Centre for Genetic Engineering and Biotechnology (ICGEB) in Trieste and New Delhi, with finance from the respective host governments, as a centre of excellence in the field, to contribute to capability building in the developing world with training, research and technology transfer. Over forty countries, most of them developing ones, have become members of ICGEB. ICGEB has since become an autonomous intergovernmental organization with ratification of its statute by twenty-six countries. It has trained over 900 scientists from thirty-five developing countries in the first five years of its existence. It has already developed a diagnostic kit for AIDS, a hepatitis-B vaccine, and insulin, all which are to be commercialized by private companies. Among other things, work is also being done on enhancing insect-resistant transgenic rice plants. Any new technologies developed at ICGEB, even if protected by an ICGEB-owned patent, will be made available to the member countries (*Biotechnology and Development Monitor*, 14, March 1993, p. 21).

FAO has been involved in evolving international conventions for the conservation and access of plant genetic resources since the early 1980s. The Convention on Biological Diversity was signed at the UN Conference on Environment and Development (UNCED) in 1992 to ensure conservation of biological diversity, sustainable use of its components and sharing the benefits equitably. However, several underlying issues remain to be settled, such as finances, intellectual property rights and patents, technological assessment, *ex-situ* gene banks and biosafety. Since it is impossible to control the spread of genetically engineered microbes once released into the environment, a code of conduct to ensure environmentally safe applications is critical. Such a code has to be internationally applicable in view of the environment being an issue of global concern. However, there has been no agreement on this issue as yet. Most developing countries insist that a protocol be negotiated to ensure an international code of conduct. Developed nations, especially those with large biotechnology industries, feel that national and private regulations are sufficient (UNEP, *Our Planet*, 6(4) 1994, p. 4).

The network of International Agricultural Research Centres (IARCs) operating under the umbrella of the Consultative Group on International Agricultural Research (CGIAR) has spearheaded the Green Revolution. IARCs have built up considerable capability in plant breeding. Biotechnologies can be valuable for their plant breeding programmes by overcoming barriers of sexual incompatibility, especially in developing varieties with a broad spectrum of resistance to pests and diseases, tolerance to adverse soil factors, and greater genetic capacity to utilize soil nitrogen. IARCs can play an important role in channelling the benefits of the biotechnology revolution to developing countries through crop improvement and also through the development of local capability, because they have already established linkages with national agricultural research systems (Kumar, 1988). Some IARCs have already moved into biotechnology. CIAT, CIMMYT, CIP, IBPGR, ICARDA, IRRI, ICRISAT, IITA and ILARD reportedly have active programmes in agriculture biotechnology (UN, 1992: 363). The funding constraints appear to be responsible for their rather slow response to the biotechnology revolution – the funding of IARCs has stagnated since the mid-1980s. In order for IARCs to develop and create the infrastructure for harnessing biotechnology in their work and to contribute to capability building in developing countries, they need to be supported by the international community by way of funding and participation.

Finally, there is considerable scope for South–South and regional cooperation in the area. Kumar (1988) has highlighted certain directions in which cooperation among developing countries could be most fruitful. These include sharing experiences in institution building, human resources development, coordination in access to basic scientific information, genetic conservation and utilization, joint research, and solidarity in North–South negotiations. Some initiatives have already been launched under the auspices of the Group of 77, the Group of 15, and regional associations such as SAARC. These need to be strengthened and more of them taken up.

CONCLUSION

The foregoing discussion has demonstrated that biotechnologies have tremendous developmental potential. The emerging character of the biotechnology industry in industrialized countries does not allow exploitation of its potential for developing countries. Developing countries need to take immediate steps to build local capacity to harness the potential of these technologies for solving their specific problems. Encouraging experiences from a number of developing countries that embarked on building capability in the area are now available. These experiences could be useful for those preparing to become involved in the area. It is quite clear from these instances that governments of developing countries have to play a critical role in promoting biotechnology capability in the country by creating an appropriate institutional infrastructure and an enabling environment before the private sector can start taking an active role. Although it has to be largely a national effort, international cooperation has to play a crucial role, especially in view of the emerging trend of the declining flow of scientific information through professional channels. International Agricultural Research Centres have played an important role in diffusing the Green Revolution to developing countries. These centres could also play an important role in exploiting the potential of biotechnology for development by using it in their breeding programmes and by training scientists from developing countries. Finally, we have noted the scope for cooperation among the developing countries – at regional and interregional levels – in building capabilities.

Part II

TECHNOLOGY AND MARKET STRUCTURE

This part discusses the role of domestic determinants of the technological effort of national enterprises. These include firm size, market structure, technological opportunities, appropriability and demand conditions. Chapter 4 deals with firm size and reviews the issues raised in theoretical and empirical literature with respect to the role of firm size in determining innovative activities and their policy implications. Chapter 5 discusses the role of market structure and other factors, their treatment in the literature, and its implications. Chapter 6 discusses the role of the technological effort of enterprises in determining their profit and growth performance, the conceptual and analytical difficulties faced by empirical studies, and the policy implications.

4

FIRM SIZE AND TECHNOLOGICAL ACTIVITY

INTRODUCTION

The role of firm size in determining innovative activity has been one of the most extensively debated issues in the theoretical and empirical literature on economics of innovation (see, among others, Kamien and Schwartz, 1982; Dosi, 1988; Cohen and Levin, 1989; Cohen, 1995, for reviews of the literature). It also happens to be one of the issues that is yet to be satisfactorily resolved because of conflicting findings in the empirical studies. This is partly because the role of size in determining R&D and other innovative activities has been a complex one. To start with, innovative activity itself has been difficult to define. Some studies have considered the inputs to innovative activities like expenditures on R&D as indicators or surrogates for innovative activity, and others have preferred some measure of R&D output, for example patents obtained, as a better representative of innovative activity. Both these measures have their limitations (see, for example, Freeman, 1982; Cohen and Levin, 1989). The main drawback of patent data is that their numbers may not truly capture innovative content, as the value of the patents could differ widely. R&D expenditures only partially represent the expenditures on technology, as expenditures on technology purchases – which could be substantial, especially in developing countries – are not covered, although the two could be related in some cases. Furthermore, informal innovative activity such as that taking place on the shop floor could be an important source of technological learning but is not captured by R&D expenditure. One of the possible reasons for the conflicting results relating to the relationship between size and innovative activity could be the diverging measurements used to denote innovative activity used by different studies.

Another factor that may have contributed to the conflicting results could be the changing nature of technological development. The technologies associated with heavy engineering, metals and petrochemical industries had substantial threshold-level size advantages with regard to R&D, while in industries based on the new core technologies such as microelectronics and biotechnology, R&D may not have size advantages. Under these conditions the R&D intensities could be high even for small firms. Finally, the diverging results could also be due to specification errors and sample selection biases in the models employed by these studies, as will be seen later.

The Schumpeterian hypothesis is discussed in the next section, and following that, the empirical evidence for the hypothesis, especially from developing countries, is examined. The chapter goes on to discuss the effect of firm size on the decision to invest in R&D, as distinguished from the intensity of R&D expenditure. Next, the effect of firm size on the nature of R&D is discussed; and the chapter closes with an examination of policy implications.

THE SCHUMPETERIAN HYPOTHESIS

Although a positive relationship between firm size and innovative activity is attributed to Schumpeter, it has been argued that Schumpeter was 'primarily impressed by the qualitative differences between the innovative activities of small, entrepreneurial enterprises and those of large, modern corporations with formal R&D laboratories' (Cohen, 1995: 184). Yet the empirical studies have tended to expect a linear continuous relationship between firm size and intensity of innovative activity, attributing it to Schumpeter. Over the years many arguments have been offered in support of a favourable effect of firm size on innovation. Galbraith (1952) argued that firm size confers an advantage in innovation in view of its rising cost. Larger firms may have an advantage in conducting innovative activity in view of a possible minimum size or threshold level below which R&D expenditures might not be efficient; and they may have an advantage in raising funds for highly risky activities such as innovation from either internal or external means given the imperfections of the capital market. Nelson and Winter (1982: 349) argue that 'the larger a firm, the greater the ability to appropriate returns from its own successful R&D efforts'. Furthermore, larger and more diversified firms may find innovative activities more fruitful because of the significant economies of scope involved.

On the other hand, if there are substantial economies of scale in R&D then expenditures on R&D need not increase in proportion to increase in the size of the firm. In other words, R&D intensity, i.e. the proportion of R&D to total sales, could in fact decline with the increase in firm size. Furthermore, Schumpeter also recognized the negative effects of bureaucratization on the efficiency of R&D as corporations grow big.

These counter arguments make a straightforward testing of the hypothesis difficult. For instance, if minimum threshold levels are present, then R&D units would not be set up below that level, as they would not then be efficient. It is also possible that smaller firms set up R&D units without information on the threshold scale. In such cases it can be expected that

R&D expenditures would increase more than proportionately with size up to the threshold level and less than proportionately beyond it.

In this context it is meaningful to make a distinction between two decisions, namely, to start an R&D unit, and the relative scale of R&D once undertaken – or R&D intensity. This differentiation could be useful because the size variable may influence the decision to start an R&D unit more favourably due to threshold advantages rather than the relative scale or intensity of R&D once set up. Most empirical studies have been confined to samples of only those firms that report R&D activities while analysing the relationship between firm size and R&D, and were unable to explain the decision-making pertaining to starting the R&D activity. These studies were also subject to obvious sample selection bias. Notable exceptions in this respect are studies by Cohen *et al.* (1987), Braga and Willmore (1991), Siddharthan and Agarwal (1992) and Kumar and Saqib (1996).

FIRM SIZE AND R&D ACTIVITY: EMPIRICAL EVIDENCE

Many of the early studies generally used linear regression to examine the relationship between some measure of firm size and a measure of innovative activity. As argued in the previous section, Schumpeter did not envisage a simple linear relationship between innovative activity and firm size. The relationship between these variables is possibly more complex. Some of the studies of the mid-1960s found R&D intensities to increase with firm size (see, for example, Comanor, 1967). Although the relationships were not strong, they were interpreted as confirmation of the so-called 'Schumpeterian' hypothesis. Mansfield (1964), however, did not find a positive relationship between these two variables. Scherer's (1965) was the first study to verify non-linearities in the relationship by including a cubic term in the function for a sample of 448 of the largest firms in 1955. He found a more than proportionate increase in innovative activities up to a threshold size and a proportionate relationship beyond that size. Thus for the first time the notion of a threshold level was verified. He also found significant differences in the relationship between size and innovative activity for different industries. For instance, he found that, for the chemical industry and for larger automobile and steel corporations, R&D intensity increased with size. One of the reasons for the industry-specific nature of the relationship could be the differences in threshold levels between industries.

The 'U'-shaped nature of size–R&D relationship, i.e. higher R&D intensities for both very small and very large firms, has also been reported by a number of recent studies (see, for example, Bound *et al.*, 1984; Acs and Audretsch, 1987, 1988). Pavitt *et al.* (1987), using output indicator for R&D, also found that both very small and very large firms were responsible for a disproportionate share of innovations.

On the relationship between firm size and R&D, the two studies by Acs and Audretsch (1987, 1988) are notable for their detailed analysis. Their results showed that large firms were not more innovative than their smaller counterparts in every industry. In fact these studies indicated that, while large firms proved to be more innovative in a number of industries, the opposite was true in certain others. With regard to the relative innovative advantage of large and small firms, they identified three factors that could influence innovative activity. These are: first, size distribution of firms; second, barriers to entry; and third, the stage of the industry in the product life cycle. They hypothesized that large firms would have an advantage in concentrated markets with significant entry barriers, while small firms would have an innovative advantage in markets that resemble a competitive market structure. Though their results, by and large, supported their hypothesis, the level of statistical significance of the coefficients was not strong.

Not many studies have analysed the relationship between firm size and technological activities in the developing countries' context, given the relatively little importance attached to enterprise-level technological activities in most of these countries. Those that pursued this link for developing countries also report similarly varying results. Lall (1983) found R&D intensity to increase with firm size more than proportionately for a cross-section sample of Indian engineering firms. Lall attributed this result to the fact that the larger firms tended to be more diversified, technologically more complex, better aware of technological opportunities, and able to afford more investment in R&D activities. Katrak (1985) postulated R&D expenditure to increase with firm size less than proportionately in view of scale economies. His results for a cross-section of Indian industries confirmed his hypothesis that the elasticity of R&D expenditures with regard to firm size was less than one.

In view of the non-linearities in the relationship observed by industrialized country studies, as reviewed above, Siddharthan (1988) postulated and found a non-linear 'U'-shaped relationship between R&D intensity and size for a cross-section sample of 166 Indian firms. Thus, for the smaller firms, R&D expenditures increased more slowly than the increase in firm size, but for the very large firms they increased more rapidly than the increase in size. This result was attributed to the differences in the nature of R&D activity undertaken by large and small firms. In addition to estimating regression equations for all the 166 firms in the sample, that included both public and private sector firms, the study also estimated equations for the private sector firms separately to analyse the differential behaviour of these two groups of firms. Furthermore, these equations were also estimated for firms belonging to different industrial groups like chemicals, electrical and electronics, industrial machinery, and textiles. In addition to the size variable, the equations also had other determinants, such as technology imports and age of the R&D units. The 'U'-shaped relationship between size and R&D intensity held good for all the equations, irrespective of the ownership group or the industrial sector. The equations showed that R&D intensity decreased with the increase in firm size, till the size of the firms in terms of sales turnover reached a certain level, and then increased beyond that. This result was valid for the combined sample of both public and private sector units, as well as for the sample consisting of only private sector units. Given the fact that the sample included very small firms as well as giant corporations, the finding of a statistically significant 'U'-shaped relationship between size and R&D intensity was not surprising.

In general, firms in developing countries spend very little on R&D. Expenditures relating to import of technology, in the form of lump sum, technical fee and royalty payments, dominate their expenditures on technology. Hence, it may be useful to analyse the role of firm size in influencing this expenditure. Studies using Indian data showed that the size of the firm was an important determinant of the ratio of technology imports to sales (Siddharthan and Krishna, 1994). Six hundred and forty firms were considered for the years 1987–90, operating in six broad industry groups. The sign of the sales coefficient was positive and significant except for electrical and electronic goods, automobiles, and miscellaneous industries. Braga and Willmore (1991) found that firm size significantly increased the probability of Brazilian firms purchasing technology from abroad.

Almost all the above studies, however, concentrated on samples of R&D reporting firms. Hence, their findings could be subject to sample selection bias, as indeed most studies cited above for industrialized country enterprises could be. Braga and Willmore (1991) for Brazilian enterprises, and Siddharthan and Agarwal (1992) and Kumar and Saqib (1996) for Indian enterprises, used more complete samples and analysed the probability of a firm undertaking R&D and its intensity. These studies generally found a positive influence of size on the probability and intensity of R&D, as will be seen in the following section.

Furthermore, firm size is a catch-all variable that captures the influence of a large number of factors such as product diversification, differentiation, internationalization, capital intensity, etc. Each one of these components could independently influence R&D expenditures. It would be worthwhile to separate their influence and then examine the actual effect of firm size. A significant effect of the size variable after controlling for these other variables would result from the resource advantages enjoyed by larger firms and the economies of scale advantages in R&D. Factors such as diversification and internationalization also capture financial, marketing and technological resource advantages, which diversified multinational enterprises are usually endowed with.

Some studies introduced other variables like foreign ownership, capital intensity, age of firm, and technology imports as determinants of R&D in addition to size (Siddharthan, 1992). The results reported in these studies showed that, in the presence of these variables, the size variable was not important. Certain other studies, such as Cohen and Levinthal (1989), considered a large number of variables that are in one way or another related to size in the equations explaining R&D, but the size variable was not separately introduced. None the less, size might not be important if the variables that influence size, or that are influenced by size, are separately introduced. Under these circumstances, it is important to make a choice in advance between a composite variable like size and a list of other variables that are associated with size. The choice will depend on the hypothesis to be tested. To test the Schumpeterian hypothesis it is preferable to employ size. While interpreting the size variable, however, one should be conscious of the other influences, such as multinationality, diversification, capital intensity, etc., that size could be capturing.

Some studies have used a more comprehensive framework covering dimensions like marketing, management, manufacturing and R&D while analysing inter-firm differences in R&D (see, for example, Mansfield, 1968; Rothwell *et al.*, 1974; Teece, 1986; Mowery and Rosenberg, 1989). They emphasize the interrelationship between these different factors. Given the interrelationships, mere expenditure on R&D might not enhance the innovative capacity of a firm. Freeman (1995) cites the case of the Soviet Union to show that commitment of greater resources to R&D did not by itself guarantee success. Diversification is another variable that is usually related to firm size. A number of studies have reported a positive relationship between diversification and R&D expenditures. Nelson (1959) found a strong relationship between basic research and product diversification. He attributed this result to the uncertainties in the outcome of basic research. Scherer (1965) found the index of diversification to be highly significant in his regression equations explaining innovative activity and firm size. Grabowski (1968) also found evidence in favour of diversification impelling R&D expenditures in the case of chemical and drug industries. Braga and Willmore (1991) found a significant positive effect of product diversification on the probability of a firm undertaking R&D and product development in Brazil.

FIRM SIZE AND THE DECISION TO INVEST IN R&D

As has been observed earlier, most studies examining the relationship between firm size and R&D suffered from sample selection bias by confining themselves to the R&D reporting firms (Cohen and Levin, 1989). If a sample includes firms that have R&D units as well as those that do not, a large number of observations will have zero value. That makes the ordinary least squares estimation an inappropriate procedure, as the results could be biased. As pointed out earlier in this chapter, two related but analytically distinct questions need to be examined while analysing the determinants of R&D expenditures. The first relates to the decision to have an R&D unit;

the second to the scale of R&D activity. The threshold levels of R&D activity would be an important consideration for the first decision, while economies of scale in R&D may affect the scale of R&D activity. Firm size could, therefore, be expected to influence the first decision favourably, but not necessarily the second one. Recent studies have attempted, with the help of appropriate models, to take care of the sampling bias and possibly the diverging influence of firm size on the probability to undertake R&D.

Cohen *et al.* (1987), using the US Federal Trade Commission's Line of Business Programme and survey measures of technological opportunity and appropriability conditions in the framework of tobit and probit models, found that overall firm size had a very small and statistically insignificant effect on business unit R&D intensity when industry effects or characteristics were taken into account. The business unit's size was found to be affecting, positively and significantly, the probability of conducting R&D, although neither measure of size influenced the R&D intensity.

Among the developing country studies, Braga and Willmore (1991) estimated a logit model for a sample of 4,342 establishments, explaining the probability of having an R&D unit or a systematic programme of product development. Firm size favourably influenced the likelihood of an establishment having R&D activity and programme development activity, even when a number of other factors and industry effects were controlled for.

Siddharthan and Agarwal (1992) considered a sample of Indian manufacturing firms drawn from the top 500 firms quoted on stock exchanges. Of the 384 firms included in the sample, only 164 firms reported R&D units. First, the authors used a probit model to explain the decision of the firms to invest in R&D in terms of firm size (with the expectation of a positive sign), and other firm and industry characteristics. Later on they analysed the determinants of R&D intensity of R&D performing firms using a separate equation. In view of the economies of scale, a negative coefficient of the firm size variable was posited. As expected, the firm size variable had a statistically significant positive coefficient in the probit model. On the other hand, firm size came up with a significantly negative coefficient in the model explaining R&D intensity. Therefore, firm size influenced the probability of a firm having R&D activity favourably, but not its intensity.

Kumar and Saqib (1996) studied the R&D behaviour of a sample of 291 firms having foreign collaborations in India. Their sample also covered both firms that had R&D units and those that did not. They employed two different models to explain R&D decisions. The first, a probit model where the dependent variable took values of either zero or one, and the second, a tobit model where firms without R&D units had zero values and those with R&D units took the actual R&D intensity. Their findings with regard to the relationship between R&D and firm size are interesting and are different from those obtained by other studies. Controlling for other determinants of R&D activity, the coefficient of size was positive and that of its quadratic term was negative, while both were statistically significant in the probit estimation. They inferred from this that the probability of undertaking R&D activity increased with firm size up to a point, beyond which it declined. In the tobit model, where the actual R&D intensities were considered as a dependent variable, while the coefficient of the size variable was positive and significant, the quadratic term was negative but not statistically significant. Based on this they concluded that, once a firm has decided to set up an R&D unit, the intensity of R&D expenditures increased with size in a linear fashion. In other words, larger firms spent more on R&D compared to smaller firms. This second result contradicted the findings of earlier works that found evidence in favour of economies of scale advantages. One of the reasons for the differences between Kumar and Saqib's results and the results of other studies could be the inclusion of both types of firms (both R&D and non-R&D firms) in their tobit model. Nevertheless the probit model results were as hypothesized and in accordance with the theoretical expectations discussed earlier. Kumar and Saqib (1992) also included a number of other explanatory variables in their models explaining firms' innovation behaviour in addition to firm size. They found export orientation and vertical integration of the firm to influence favourably both the probability and intensity of R&D activity.

To summarize the above discussion, therefore, firm size is more likely to determine the likelihood of a firm's tendency to undertake R&D activity rather than the scale of that activity. The scale or intensity of R&D may depend on other factors, including industry characteristics and indeed the size profile of the sample firms. In view of the diverging results with respect to influence of firm size in explaining probability and intensity of R&D found by all these studies, findings of earlier studies need to be re-examined. Furthermore, it is also becoming quite clear that the relationships vary across industry groups depending upon the extent of scale economies involved in R&D activity in different industries.

FIRM SIZE AND THE NATURE OF R&D

A number of studies done in the 1980s suggested a possible 'U'-shaped nature of the relationship between firm size and R&D, i.e. both small and large firms in the industry have expenditure on R&D despite the existence of threshold advantages. One explanation of this finding could be that the nature of R&D undertaken by small and large firms is different and therefore not comparable. If large and small firms belong to two different strategic groups undertaking different types of R&D work, then it is quite conceivable that there would be two different threshold levels for these two groups – a lower threshold level for a certain type of R&D work, mostly adaptive and resulting in minor changes, and a higher threshold level for other kinds of R&D. If this is true, then smaller firms could have higher

R&D intensities (though in terms of absolute expenditures they might not be large), and an increase in firm size would result in a less than proportionate increase in R&D expenditures due to the presence of scale economies. But beyond a certain size, firms could aim at the second threshold and change the nature of their R&D work. This would result in a more than proportionate increase in R&D expenditures to increase in firm size until the second threshold level is reached. In that case the relationship between R&D intensities and firm size would be 'U'-shaped.

A few studies have indeed reported differences in the nature and composition of R&D undertaken by small and large firms. The results of these studies indicate that larger firms carried out more process R&D compared to smaller firms (Mansfield, 1981; Pavitt *et al.*, 1987; Scherer, 1991). In support of these results they argue that, given the large turnover of the giant corporations, more is gained by introducing incremental process innovations into existing lines of operations rather than by introducing risky product innovations with uncertain future turnovers. However, this argument could not hold good for all industries.

It is possible to explain the observation of relatively high R&D intensities in both small and large firms using the neo-Schumpeterian framework. The neo-Schumpeterians (e.g. Dosi, 1988) make a distinction between technological paradigms and trajectories. Technological paradigms refer to major technological and manufacturing configurations. These paradigms do not change frequently, and when they do, the change could have a major impact on the industry. On the other hand, trajectory shifts refer to small incremental changes introduced by the firms themselves in response to market conditions and the firms' own technological capabilities. These incremental changes are endogenous in nature. Two firms could be operating in the same technological paradigm but could have very different trajectories (Metcalfe, 1995). It is possible that the larger firms focus their R&D activities on shifting or changing the paradigms, while the smaller firms concentrate mainly on technological trajectories. Since trajectory shifts are primarily incremental and evolutionary in nature, they may not require massive R&D expenditures and huge units. These could be within the reach of the smaller firms. However, the impact of the trajectory shifts on the firms' performance could be substantial. Evidence indicates that, in several medium technology industries, smaller Indian firms did influence the trajectories through in-house R&D, factory floor improvements, and learning by doing (Ito, 1986). In the case of new technologies like biotechnology and micro-electronics, however, there are not substantial size advantages in R&D and consequently even smaller firms could contribute to product development and bring about major changes. A combination of these two factors could explain the high R&D intensities in both small and large firms.

CONCLUDING REMARKS AND POLICY IMPLICATIONS

This chapter has discussed the theoretical and empirical issues involved in analysing the role of firm size in determining the technological activity of firms. Firm size has been expected to favour innovative activity in the literature of the neo-Schumpeterian tradition. However, findings from a rather large body of empirical literature for industrialized countries have been diverging, possibly because of varying methodologies employed by the studies, specification and sampling errors, and also because of the possibly different nature of technological activities between larger and smaller firms. The bulk of the literature has failed to distinguish between the two decisions involved which may be affected by firm size differently, i.e. the decision to undertake R&D and the scale of R&D activity once started.

The studies for developing countries generally suggest that larger firms are more likely to have an R&D unit or formal technological activity than smaller firms, although the intensity of R&D activity might not always be affected positively by firm size, given the economies of scale in technological activity and depending upon the composition of the sample. There is a strong possibility of the relationship between firm size and R&D being subject to non-linearity. Therefore, evidence for developing countries highlights the role of firm size in technological effort, unlike a somewhat inconclusive finding reached by industrialized country literature (see Cohen, 1995). Given the economies of scale in R&D, the productivity of the technological effort of larger firms may be higher because of the larger scale of their R&D. Therefore, the evidence would tend to support policies that encourage larger national enterprises to take a greater role in building the technological capabilities of the nation. While the technological activities of small and medium enterprises are important, especially in new technologies, and should be encouraged, it is the technological activities of the larger national enterprises that can make a visible difference to the national technological capabilities. Japan and Korea were able to build highly competitive technological capabilities by encouraging the technological activities of their larger enterprises. The national technological capabilities in different sectors of different countries are indeed reflected in the relative capabilities of their respective national champions, e.g. General Electric for capability in electrical engineering in the USA, Philips for electronics capability in the Netherlands, Daimler for transportation equipment and Hoechst or Bayer for chemical technology in Germany, Sony for consumer electronics and Toyota for automobiles in Japan, Samsung for semiconductors and electronics in Korea, to name but a few. The recent wave of corporate restructuring involving mergers between giant MNEs, e.g. ASEA and Brown Boveri, Glaxo and Wellcome, Sandoz and Ciba-Geigy, has largely been motivated by the need to take advantage of the economies of scale in R&D activity and of synergies in their competences. It may be fruitful for developing countries to focus their efforts on building technological capability in select areas by encouraging larger national enterprises to build their own technological capabilities to enable them to make increasingly independent technological choices. Vertical inter-firm linkages between larger enterprises and smaller firms may be encouraged in order to allow for wider diffusion of technology within the economy through traditional vendor–customer links. From the perspective of building local technological capability, therefore, a corporate consolidation of larger enterprises may be more conducive than the fragmentation of production capability into numerous small enterprises. One should keep in mind, however, that firm size is only one of several determinants of technological innovations. Furthermore, a high level of concentration of economic activity in a few big corporations may have other undesirable socio-economic consequences, a discussion of which is beyond the scope of this book. This, however, is a trade-off to be resolved by the governments in line with the goals of their development policy.

5

MARKET STRUCTURE, OPPORTUNITIES, PATENTS AND INNOVATIONS

INTRODUCTION

Market structure has also been posited as an important influence on the technological activity of enterprises in the literature of the Schumpeterian tradition. In addition, the literature has emphasized the role of technological opportunities and appropriability conditions in determining the innovative activities of enterprises. This chapter summarizes the issues raised in the literature, especially in the developing country context.

The next section discusses the theoretical issues raised in the literature on the market structure–innovation relationship. The following section reviews the empirical literature on market structure and innovation from both industrialized and developing countries, and examines their limitations. Following this, the role of appropriability conditions and patents in determining the innovative activities of technological opportunities of firms is discussed. The chapter goes on to summarize the literature on the influence of technological opportunities on innovative activities, and the recent refinements made in the concept are discussed in a developing country context. Finally, the chapter concludes with some implications for policy.

THE SCHUMPETERIAN PARADIGM

Schumpeter was among the first to relate market structure to innovative activity. He argued that a perfectly competitive market structure was not conducive to innovative activity. A competitive market structure is one where a large number of small firms compete in a given product market and where the share of each firm in the total output is negligible. Under this condition no firm will be able to influence the price of the product by varying its output as it contributes only an insignificant portion of the total output. Nor can the firms collude together, form a cartel and influence the market prices, as there are too many firms in the market for an effective collusion. Furthermore, under perfect competition, information regarding technology and other factors is freely available to all the firms as well as to the prospective entrants. These characteristics ensure free entry and exit of the firms to and from the product market. Given these conditions one can easily show that all firms operating under this market structure would earn only normal profits in the long run. Any super-normal profits in the short run will not last, as new firms would enter the market, increase the supply and bring the profits down to the normal level. Furthermore, in the long run the firms would produce at the minimum point on the average cost curve where the price of the product is equal not only to the marginal cost but also to the average cost.

The other extreme of perfect competition is the situation of monopoly, where the firm and the market coincide as only one firm exists in the product market. This single firm can influence prices by varying its output, as its output is the market's output. If it so desires, the firm can increase prices by reducing its output and creating scarcity conditions. It can also be shown that the firm will fix the quantity of its output in a manner such that the extra revenue it gets through the production of that output is equal to the extra cost of producing it, that is, it equates its marginal cost to marginal revenue. It can further be demonstrated that firms that equate their marginal cost to price will produce more compared to firms that equate their marginal cost to marginal revenue. Consequently, textbooks on the theory of the firm argue that the monopoly market structure is anti-welfare, exploitative (monopoly price is higher than competitive price) and anti-growth (monopoly output is lower than competitive output). Accordingly, most governments oppose monopoly and have enacted legislation to curb monopoly tendencies. The US has anti-trust laws, while the UK, India and many other countries have anti-monopoly laws and regulations to control the emergence of monopolies.

Schumpeter (1942) disagreed with the traditional theories on monopoly. The traditional view that the monopoly price is higher and monopoly output lower is true only if the method and the organization of production and everything else are assumed to be exactly the same as in perfect competition. But according to Schumpeter (1942: 100), 'Actually . . . there are superior methods available to the monopolists which either are not available at all to a crowd of competitors or are not available to them so readily.' This is so mainly because the monopoly firm, unlike a competitive firm, is able to generate a surplus (super-normal profits) which it can invest in R&D and other innovative activities. Through these it can create new processes and differentiated products and methods of production that would lower the cost curves. A competitive firm, on the other hand, has no surpluses to invest in innovative activities. Given these differences, the monopolist's cost curve and product profiles are not comparable to those of a competitive firm.

A firm could acquire monopoly status through government interventions such as industrial approvals and other forms of direct control. Monopoly acquired through such procedures could result in exploitation, as is alluded to in the textbooks. Monopoly status could also be acquired through investments in innovative activities resulting in the creation of new technologies, new methods of production and new products. Monopoly due to the creation and ownership of intangible assets, in the form of technology, etc., cannot last for ever, as other firms could compete in technology creation and succeed in creating a better technology or a better product. This would bring down the profits of the monopolists. Hence, Schumpeter (1942: 102) stated, 'a monopoly position is in general no cushion to sleep on. As it can be gained, so it can be retained only by alertness and energy . . . Thus it is true that there is or may be an element of genuine monopoly gain in those entrepreneurial profits which are the prizes offered by capitalist society to the successful innovator. But the quantitative importance of the element, its volatile nature and its function in the process in which it emerges put it in a class by itself.'

Moreover, to Schumpeter (1942: 105), 'The introduction of new methods of production and new commodities is hardly conceivable with perfect competition from the start. And this means that the bulk of what we call economic progress is incompatible with it.' Consequently, Schumpeter did not agree with the view that large enterprises and less than perfectly competitive market structures are necessary evils of modern methods of production. Instead it is important to recognize that they have come to be the most powerful engines of progress. Hence he was categorically against all governmental regulations of industry on the principle that big business should be made to work as the respective industry would work in perfect competition.

The argument, that the perfectly competitive market structure is not conducive for innovative activities because it does not generate resources for investment in such ventures and because the small size of the firms in that market structure will not be able to meet the minimum threshold level investments, does not necessarily lead to the conclusion that the monopoly market structure is ideal for innovative activities. Many of the oligopolistic firms are also capable of generating resources for R&D. Schumpeterian arguments in fact point towards imperfectly competitive market structures rather than a pure monopoly, though Schumpeter himself did not emphasize this point. In practice most of the empirical studies have examined a relationship between industrial concentration and R&D expenditures in verification of the Schumpeterian hypothesis.

EMPIRICAL STUDIES ON MARKET STRUCTURE AND INNOVATION

The empirical verification of Schumpeter's postulate, that concentrated market structures are more conducive for innovative activities than competitive ones, has generally been made in the literature by positing a positive influence of the degree of seller concentration (generally measured in terms of four- or eight-firm concentration ratios) on innovative behaviour in the industry. The findings of these studies have been mixed, leading Cohen and Levin (1989) to conclude that concentration *per se* might not exercise any independent influence on R&D. Mansfield (1968) and Scherer (1965, 1967) found a positive, though weak, relationship between market concentration and R&D intensity. Comanor (1967), Phillips (1966) and Shrieves (1978) found the influence of market structure on innovation to be dependent upon other factors, such as product differentiation and technological opportunity. Comanor argued that, in the presence of entry barriers, concentration does not encourage innovation.

Among the developing country studies, Desai (1983), on the basis of an examination of the relationship between market structure and technological activities in Indian industries and also several industry case studies, concluded that market structures with few firms – between two and half a dozen – were more conducive to adoption of new technology by firms and that 'the long tailed market structures common in India are not especially conducive to technological progress; nor are the monopoly firms set up by the government in high-technology industries'. Kumar (1987b), in a study of forty-three Indian manufacturing industries, found a negative influence of four-firm concentration ratio on R&D intensity. He explained this finding in terms of government policy factors which deterred entry to industry in addition to the structural barriers to entry. The entry to Indian industries until recently had been regulated by the government through its industrial licensing policy. The competition from abroad had been shielded by tariffs, non-tariff barriers and exchange controls. The existing firms, therefore, faced hardly any threat or potential competition. The principal motivation for firms to pursue innovative activity is to acquire monopoly power with the accompanying quasi rents. He therefore argued, like Comanor, that in the absence of any threat of potential competition high concentration does not provide any motivation for innovation.

Braga and Willmore (1991), for a sample of 4,342 establishments in Brazil, found that the extent of concentration (measured in terms of Herfindahl index) affected the likelihood of a firm having a specific programme of product development positively up to an extent beyond which it affected the likelihood adversely. Hence, the relationship was of an inverted 'U'-shape.

Since the early 1980s a number of studies have stressed a two-way relationship between market structure and R&D (see, for instance, Dasgupta and Stiglitz, 1980; Nelson and Winter, 1982; Levin and Reiss, 1984). Levin and Reiss have argued that a truly Schumpeterian framework requires that both market structure and R&D be treated as endogenous variables, as Schumpeter's notion of 'creative destruction' emphasized that market structure is influenced by past and current innovative successes and failures.

Furthermore, the market power generated by innovation is transient and is eroded by rival innovation and imitation. The evolutionary theory of Nelson and Winter (1982: 350–1) predicts that industries with rapid technical progress ought to be marked by high average R&D intensity and, as the industry matures, by a more concentrated industry structure than industries in which technical progress is slower, and that concentration is likely to increase over time in a technologically progressive industry. The empirical literature has been rather slow to respond to the need of specifying market structure as an endogenous variable. A few attempts have been made in the direction of taking care of the endogeneity problem in the framework of simultaneous models.

Farber (1981) made a number of analytical improvements. First, he considered the simultaneity in the relationship between market structure and innovation. Second, he introduced a non-linear relationship between concentration and R&D intensity, and in particular, he introduced a quadratic term for the concentration variable. Third, and in some respects, most important, he also considered buyer concentration which had been neglected by most of the studies. His major finding was that R&D activities were high in industries that had both buyer and seller concentration, and not merely buyer or seller concentration. In his equations buyer and seller concentration variables had negative signs, but the interaction variable, namely the interaction of buyer and seller concentration, had a significant positive sign. Farber rationalized his results with the help of arguments connecting appropriability, rates of adoption and R&D intensity. He predicted an increase in R&D intensity with increased buyer concentration only if accompanied by increased seller concentration and not otherwise. If the buyer concentration was high and the seller concentration not, or vice versa, it would have a negative impact on appropriability and rates of adoption. Appropriability conditions would be fulfilled only in a market structure where there were few buyers and sellers; or where the seller market structure was oligopolistic and the buyer market structure was oligopsonistic.

Levin and Reiss (1984), using the National Science Foundation data for a panel of twenty industries over three points of time found a significant and negative influence of Herfindahl index measure of concentration on R&D intensity in the presence of two interactive terms of concentration, i.e. one with the intensity of product development in industry R&D and government funding of R&D. In the absence of these interactive terms the concentration variable had a positive sign but was not statistically significant. Therefore, the influence of market structure seems to be dependent upon other factors, as many other studies have reported. On the other hand, concentration was significantly increased by a variable obtained by adding the R&D and advertisement intensities. Connolly and Hirschey (1984), in another attempt to examine the relationship between R&D intensity and market structure in the framework of a simultaneous equations model for a sample of 390 of the

Fortune 500 corporations, also reported positive influences of concentration, technological opportunity and profitability on R&D intensity. They also found R&D intensity and advertising intensity to increase concentration. Geroski and Pomroy (1990) argued that the current technological change was decentralizing and would decrease concentration. Their main hypothesis was 'competition stimulates innovation and innovation increases the degree of competition in markets, both effects leading in principle to a steady rise in the rate of innovation and to a steady fall in the market concentration over time' (p. 300). In an examination of the impact of a wide range of innovations on market concentration for a cross-section of seventy-three UK industries for the years 1970–9, they found the innovative activity to be affecting the evolution of market structures and leading to deconcentration. But these results are not comparable to those of studies cited earlier, as the focus is on examination of the effect of innovations introduced in an industry on concentration levels rather than the effect of innovations of enterprises on the market structure in the industry, and vice versa.

Anglemar (1985) explored the concentration–innovation relationship further by introducing appropriability conditions and technological opportunities in a study employing a sample of 160 business units included in the PIMS database for 1978. He found that concentration in broadly defined industries had a negligible impact on R&D investment. The picture changed when concentration was measured in more appropriately defined industries and when the relative cost and uncertainty were taken into account. In industries with relatively low cost and uncertainty of R&D and strong barriers against imitation, sufficient incentives for innovation exist even in the absence of high concentration, and concentration actually tended to reduce the level of R&D intensity. Concentration, on the other hand, was important for the exploitation of technological opportunities in industries characterized by relatively high cost and uncertainty of R&D and no barriers to imitation.

These studies, therefore, suggest that the market structure's influence on innovation, besides being subject to a possible simultaneity bias, may also be dependent on other factors such as barriers to entry, appropriability and technological opportunities. Certain types of market structure promote R&D activities mainly because they facilitate appropriability.

PATENTS, APPROPRIABILITY AND R&D INTENSITIES

The main argument offered in favour of tighter and more stringent laws to protect intellectual property and patent rights is to provide better conditions for appropriability of innovations. However, the existing empirical literature suggests (see Cohen and Levin, 1989) that the effectiveness of patent protection varies from industry to industry and is most effective only in the chemical and pharmaceutical industries. A study by Mansfield (1986) showed that around 65 per cent of pharmaceutical and 30 per cent of chemical inventions would not have taken place but for patent protection. In the case of most other industries patent protection was not important. In the case of most of the engineering industries, and in particular, electrical and electronic goods and instruments, patent protection was not found to be essential for the introduction of inventions. This finding was confirmed by most of the subsequent studies. These studies also revealed that secrecy was more effective than patents in protecting process innovations. Besides, in the case of several high technology industries like aerospace and industrial machinery, the complexity of the products made reverse engineering very costly and imitation difficult, even without patent protection. Scherer and Weisburst (1995) examined the impact of strengthening of pharmaceutical patent protection in Italy since 1978. They concluded that regime change had had little or no impact on the trend of inflation-adjusted R&D expenditures or on the introduction of new chemical entities. Hence, they expressed their scepticism about the prospect that the trend of strengthening patent protection with the TRIPs agreement would significantly raise innovative activity, especially in developing countries.

Cohen and Levinthal (1989), in their comprehensive model explaining R&D intensity, considered technological opportunity as well as appropriability as determinants. While analysing the impact of appropriability on R&D intensity, they also postulated and took into account the impact of spillover effects. They also assessed the beneficial impact of spillover effects on R&D to comprehend the net outcome on R&D investments. The introduction of this new dimension is of crucial importance from the point of view of policy. One of the important determinants of R&D is technological opportunity. Technological opportunity is a function of technological and research output in that area, as well as the output of other R&D units which the patent owners wish to protect by reducing the spillover effects. On the other hand, the spillover effect is one of the notable inputs to R&D. Consequently, in analysing the impact of a lack of effective patent protection, one should also take into account the positive impact of spillover effects. Cohen and Levinthal's results showed that the positive absorption incentive associated with spillovers seemed to increase relative to the negative appropriability incentive in the case of many industries. To examine whether on balance the spillovers actually encouraged R&D in some industries, they undertook a more sophisticated analysis and found that, in the case of chemicals and electrical and electronics, R&D intensities increased with spillovers. It is striking to note that these two industries are high technology ones with high R&D intensities. Therefore, the available evidence does not indicate that further tightening of the intellectual property and patenting laws would increase expenditures on R&D. On the contrary, if one goes by the results of Cohen and Levinthal, R&D spillovers are an important input to promote R&D; hence, restricting spillovers further by tightening patent protection could hurt subsequent R&D efforts. In developing countries where much of the R&D activity is of an adaptive nature, tighter intellectual property rights might choke the innovative activity by reducing the knowledge from spillovers available to the R&D of foreign firms. A number of studies have empirically demonstrated the ability of rather weaker intellectual property rights in stimulating domestic innovative activity in developing countries to absorb spillovers of foreign R&D. Fikkert (1993), in a study of Indian enterprises, found evidence of their R&D activity absorbing considerable foreign R&D spillovers facilitated by the weak Indian patent regime, and concluded that a stronger patent regime was 'not optimal from either short- or long-term perspectives'. Similarly, Kumar and Saqib (1996) found Indian chemical industry enterprises to be among the more innovative ones in Indian industry. They attributed this to the weak patent laws, i.e. the absence of product patents in India which enabled Indian enterprises to undertake alternative process development. Enterprises in developing countries like India hardly have the physical and financial resources to engage in creative research in the chemical and drug industries. In the presence of product patents, the process adaptations such as those exhibited by the Indian chemical industry could not be undertaken. Therefore, the implications of intellectual property protection for the domestic technological effort in a country would vary according to the stage of development.

TECHNOLOGICAL OPPORTUNITY AND OPPORTUNITIES FOR ADAPTATION

It is now widely recognized that industries differ in opportunities available for innovation which themselves are dependent upon scientific advancement. Engineering industries offer a much greater opportunity of innovation than, for instance, metallurgy or textile industries. However, a precise measurement of capturing varying technological opportunities across industries has not yet been found. Most of the empirical studies used industry dummies to capture technological opportunities faced by them. Scherer (1965) classified industries based on technological opportunities and used industry dummies. In particular he considered the chemical, electrical and mechanical industries as the ones that had higher technological opportunities compared to traditional technology industries. Scherer found that about half of the total inter-industry variation in innovative activity in the US manufacturing industries could be explained in terms of these 'dynamic supply conditions' that are dependent upon broad advances of science and technological knowledge or technological opportunities.

The main disadvantage in using industry dummies to capture technological opportunity is that, in addition to technological opportunities, they can also represent other industry characteristics. Some studies have considered and developed some indicators of scientific discoveries and have used these indicators as technological opportunity variables. Scientific discoveries are of a general nature and could find their applications in more than one industry. Hence, it is difficult to associate a particular scientific discovery as contributing to the technological opportunity in an industry. Another important difficulty arises from the complexity of relationship between science and technology. While technological opportunity aids in the innovation of new products and processes, the newly invented instruments and products themselves promote research in basic sciences and technology.

Jaffe (1986) employed twenty technological opportunity clusters but found that conventional industry dummies performed equally well. Levin *et al.* (1985), Cohen *et al.* (1987) and Cohen and Levinthal (1989) introduced what they thought to be the two most important sources of technological opportunity, namely, relevance of science and the importance of extra industry sources of knowledge. A survey conducted by Levin *et al.* measured the relevance to an industry's R&D of eleven basic and applied scientific fields for each line of business. The basic sciences included biology, chemistry, geology, mathematics and physics. The applied sciences included agricultural science, applied mathematics, operational research, computer science, materials science, medical science and metallurgy. Their relevance is assessed on a seven point scale. The survey also gave information on the importance (on a seven point scale) of the contribution of various external sources of knowledge to technical progress within each line of business. It considered five sources of external knowledge: upstream suppliers of raw materials and equipment; downstream users of the industry's products; government agencies; research laboratories; and universities. Levin *et al.* developed an innovative model to make the best possible use of this information and to examine the impact of technological opportunity on R&D investments. Out of the five external sources of knowledge considered, the first two, i.e. upstream suppliers and downstream users, are more directly targeted to in-house R&D and, therefore, would be expected to be important. Cohen *et al.* (1987) found that fixed industry effects explained nearly half of the variance in R&D intensity. The measured industry characteristics constructed using the above procedure explained an additional 50 per cent variation to that explained by fixed two-digit industry effects. Cohen and Levinthal's (1989) empirical findings showed that, although the coefficients of the eleven variables representing technological opportunity associated with scientific fields were jointly significant across all the estimation methods used by them, the technological opportunity associated with the relatively less targeted basic sciences elicited more R&D spending than that associated with the applied sciences. A comparison of the coefficient magnitudes of the basic versus the applied sciences showed that, with the exception of geology in the case of basic sciences and computer science in the case of applied sciences (the two expected cases), the coefficients were uniformly greater for basic sciences (Cohen and Levinthal, 1989: 585–7). In the case of extra industry sources of knowledge, the university source had a coefficient value higher than the other four. The dominant sources of technological opportunity, therefore, appear to be the basic sciences and university research, which are not subject to patent protection.

Kumar and Saqib (1996) argued that, in developing countries such as India where the bulk of R&D activity is of an adaptive rather than a creative type, inter-industry differences in opportunities for product and process adaptation are more relevant than technological opportunities in determining the R&D strategy of enterprises. The opportunities for adaptation may vary across industries, depending, among other factors, upon the maturity of the technology, the gap between local and global standards, the degree of monopolistic hold over technology and the nature of intellectual property protection, and the need for such adaptation arising from different local conditions. The opportunities for adaptation were expected to be particularly greater in capital goods industries because of the minor design changes needed to adapt them to local conditions, or in chemical industries where the absence of product patents has encouraged Indian firms to work out alternative processes for the manufacture of known chemicals and bulk drugs. In Kumar and Saqib's empirical exercise, Indian enterprises in three industries, electrical equipment, non-electrical machinery and machine tools, and chemicals and drugs, exhibited a greater probability as well as intensity of undertaking R&D activity than other enterprises.

CONCLUDING REMARKS AND POLICY IMPLICATIONS

This chapter has reviewed the empirical and theoretical literature on the role of market structure and some other determinants of innovative activity, namely, appropriability conditions and technological opportunity. Market concentration has been expected to favour innovative activity rather than perfectly competitive market structures in the Schumpeterian tradition. The empirical literature, however, has found that the market structure's effect on innovation may be dependent upon other factors, such as technological opportunities, appropriability conditions, and entry conditions. Furthermore, the relationship may be subject to a simultaneity problem. Under certain conditions, a market structure consisting of few buyers and few sellers could be more conducive for innovation. The role of threat of entry or potential competition as a major factor in determining in-house R&D activities has also been highlighted, especially in a developing country context. A few studies that explored the other direction of causation between market structure and innovation in the framework of simultaneous equation models generally reported a positive and significant effect of R&D activity on concentration. This could be because the innovative activity of existing firms may raise barriers to the entry of new firms. Besides, the patent system also grants temporary monopolies to the firms that introduce innovations. This suggests a role for policy. National competition or anti-trust policies are needed to prevent the build-up of excessive monopoly power of certain enterprises and to ensure a constant threat of entry of new firms. The competition policy could also deal with possible abuse of monopoly power emanating from patent protection. Section 8 of the TRIPs agreement under the World Trade Organization explicitly provides for appropriate measures to prevent the abuse of intellectual property rights or the resort to anti-competitive practices.

The role of appropriability conditions in encouraging innovative activity has assumed importance in recent times with the attempt by industrialized countries to strengthen the intellectual property protection system world-wide through multilateral trade negotiations. One of the arguments in favour of a stronger regime of intellectual property is based on the premise that expenditures on R&D were significantly determined by appropriability conditions. Hence, ensuring adequate appropriability with more stringent protection of the intellectual property was deemed to be a necessary condition for sustaining the pace of innovation in the global economy. The empirical literature, however, does not support this presumption, as patent protection was found to be instrumental for only a small proportion of innovations. On the other hand, studies show the spillover effects of the R&D activity of other firms to be a lot more important than appropriability in inducing firms to undertake R&D. The R&D outputs of other firms form valuable inputs for the R&D efforts of these firms. Hence, tightening of intellectual property protection is likely to affect innovative activity adversely by stifling these spillovers. It is also likely adversely to affect the technological activity of developing country enterprises, which is largely of an adaptive nature. For instance, the process innovations which form an important part of the innovative activity of developing country enterprises in the chemical industry, for the known bulk drugs and chemicals covered by product patents, would be prevented by the new regime established by TRIPs under the World Trade Organization.

In this context it may be useful to recall that Schumpeter argued for the short-term nature of monopoly profits to encourage innovation and not for a legal institutionalized monopoly position. When he wrote that monopoly offered 'no cushion to sleep on', he emphasized the temporary state of monopoly resulting from the possession of a new technology. In the medium and long term, the firm would be subject to the threat of competition and the advent of better or improved products from rivals – hence the need for the firm to safeguard its market position through continuous innovative activities. It was this process that prevented the original creator of a new technology from being complacent and prompted the monopolist to be constantly creative. Legal protection, as provided by the patent system for the rather longer term of twenty years, therefore, erodes the threat of potential competition and, hence, the need for continuous improvement.

Technological opportunity has emerged as the most prominent variable explaining investments in R&D in empirical studies. An interesting finding of some recent studies is that the basic sciences played a more prominent role than developments in applied sciences and technologies in encouraging investment in R&D. Besides, the results of university research contributed more to R&D investments than research in the upstream component manufacturing sector or the downstream user sector. The literature has also suggested that opportunities for adaptation rather than technological opportunities may be the more relevant factors in explaining the technological activities of developing country enterprises, which are generally of an adaptive nature. These opportunities may be substantially reduced by the monopolistic hold over technologies provided by patent protection. Hence, the ongoing strengthening and harmonization of the patent system has the prospect of adversely affecting the technological activities in developing countries by reducing the opportunities for adaptation.

6

TECHNOLOGICAL ACTIVITIES, MARKET STRUCTURE AND FIRM'S PERFORMANCE

INTRODUCTION

Chapters 4 and 5 were concerned with the factors that determine the technological activities of enterprises. This chapter goes on to discuss the implications of technological activities for an enterprise's performance and related issues raised in the theoretical and empirical literature. Technological activities could influence the performance of firms by shifting the firms' demand curve to the right, as a consequence of the introduction of new or improved products or as a result of product differentiation. Process adaptations, innovations or changes in the input mix to suit local resource endowments could reduce the cost of production and shift the cost curve downwards. In either way, technological activities could improve a firm's competitiveness in the domestic and international markets and may reflect on its profit and growth performance.

Three strands of theoretical literature have related technological activities with different aspects of a firm's performance. First, in the Market Structure–Conduct–Performance (S–C–P) paradigm, the technological activity of firms is posited as an aspect of conduct or non-price rivalry, like advertisement, which firms employ to gain a competitive advantage over their rivals and also to raise barriers to the entry of potential entrants. Hence, it is expected to contribute to a firm's market power and in turn to its profit margins. The second strand of literature includes theories typified by that of Robin Marris (1964). In these models, firms employ R&D and other technological activities to remove constraints on growth in the long term. The third strand of literature includes the neo-technology theories of international trade that relate technology with trade performance. This chapter will confine itself to the first two strands of literature, leaving the third to be dealt with in Chapter 8.

The plan of the chapter is as follows. The next section discusses issues raised in the first strand of literature, i.e. the Structure–Conduct–Performance paradigm in the inter-industry context where the technology intensity of the industry is treated as an entry barrier. The empirical literature in this stream is selectively reviewed and the problems encountered by empirical studies in verifying the effect of the technology variable on industry performance are highlighted. Recent extensions of the theory intended to overcome the limitations of earlier studies in examining the effect of the technology variable are discussed. Next, inter-firm literature in the S–C–P context, which treats a firm's technological activities as aspects of competitive rivalry, is dealt with. The following section reviews the literature dealing with the role of technology in determining a firm's growth in the tradition of managerial theories. The final section concludes the chapter with some remarks on policy.

TECHNOLOGY, ENTRY BARRIERS AND INDUSTRY PROFITS

A large body of empirical literature has employed the Market Structure–Conduct–Performance paradigm (S–C–P) to explain inter-industry differences in profits since 1970. A typical model for explaining profit differences included elements of market structure, i.e. industrial concentration and entry barriers, in addition to the growth rate of demand. The literature has considered four sources of entry barriers: economies of scale; absolute cost advantage of existing firms; product differentiation; and absolute capital requirements in the Bainian tradition. Although technology did not appear explicitly to be a source of entry barrier, it could be a significant barrier especially in knowledge-intensive industries. New entrants in these industries will have either to undertake R&D activity to create technology, or procure it from someone possessing it. R&D activity is known to have substantial economies of scale and the markets for technology are known to be imperfect. Technology owners are also accorded legal protection during the life of a patent. Hence, the technology intensity of an industry could be a formidable barrier to entry (Kumar, 1990b: 83). Furthermore, technological activities, especially product innovations and adaptations, are important sources of product differentiation.

In a direct empirical examination of the determinants of entry in seventy-one Canadian manufacturing industries, Orr (1974) found technology intensity (intensity of industry in R&D and purchased technology) to be an important and statistically significant barrier to entry, along with other standard sources of entry barriers such as capital requirement, advertising intensity, etc. Technology intensity may emerge as an entry barrier of an even greater potency in a developing country context, as in most cases technology has to be sourced from international markets which are highly imperfect. However, the importance of technology or R&D intensity of an industry as an entry barrier has been somewhat neglected by the vast body of literature that has emerged over time on determinants of inter-industry variation in profits, as is clear from recent surveys. For instance, an extensive survey of the literature on inter-industry studies of structure and performance by Schmalensee (1989) does not even raise the possibility that technology or

R&D intensity might play a role in explaining industry profits as an entry barrier. Another survey, that of Hay and Morris (1991), recognizes the possibility of R&D constituting another barrier via its effect on cost structure, and cites the studies of Mansfield and Levin suggesting the potential of R&D constituting 'a more persistent type of barrier' (Hay and Morris, 1991: 230). But the relative neglect of R&D or technology intensity as an entry barrier by the empirical literature surveyed by Hay and Morris is apparent, especially with reference to a table that summarizes the empirical studies on industrial profitability (Table 8A.1, pp. 262–7). Of the sixty-seven studies from different countries summarized in this table, only a handful (seven) included R&D intensity as one of the explanatory variables, and in five of these studies the variable came up with a significant coefficient with the expected positive sign. Among the developing country studies, Siddharthan and Dasgupta (1983), for a sample of thirty Indian industries, found R&D intensity of industry insignificant in explaining profit differences.

One of the reasons for the relative neglect of the R&D or technology intensity variable by empirical studies is the difficulty in obtaining reliable indicators of technology intensity, as, unlike other variables, technology variables are seldom reported in company accounts, especially in developing countries. The measurement of technology intensity is subject to several errors which may lead to poor results, hence discouraging scholars from testing and reporting it. These errors may be on several accounts. For one, because technological purchases from abroad account for a substantial proportion of the technology employed in industry in most countries, the R&D carried out by the domestic industry may not represent the technology intensity of the industry. Caves *et al.* (1980) recognized this point while arguing that 'R&D of the sort carried out in Canada . . . serve the defensive purpose of adapting knowledge originated abroad to Canadian conditions or fortifying Canadian companies against international competition'. Under that argument they postulated an inverse relationship between the R&D intensity of Canadian industry and profitability. They employed another variable representing the R&D intensity of the corresponding industry in the US, weighted by the share of US affiliates in Canadian industry. This variable had the predicted positive sign and was statistically significant. Orr (1974) and Kumar (1990b), among others, used the sum of local R&D and expenditure on technology purchase abroad by the local industry as the variable representing the technology intensity of the industry.

Finally, entry barriers such as technology intensity and product differentiation may affect firms within an industry differently in the light of the strategic groups hypothesis proposed by Caves and Porter (1977). If that is so, the relationship between the technology intensity of an industry and average profitability may be insignificant or weak, holding good only for specific strategic groups within the industry. The strategic groups and mobility barriers hypothesis is actually an extension of the S–C–P paradigm which enables an explanation of intra-industry profit differences. The S–C–P paradigm offers no explanation of intra-industry profitability differences because it relates profitability to the degree of concentration and the height of entry barriers. Since the entry barriers are industry specific, they are expected to protect all firms in the industry. This is an important limitation, as it is common to observe sustained intra-industry profitability differences. Caves and Porter (1977) sought to provide an explanation of sustained intra-industry differences in profitability in terms of the strategic heterogeneity of firms.

Caves and Porter argued that there are alternative ways of doing business and that the strategy of firms in a particular industry differs in respect of variables besides scale, such as mode of competitive rivalry, degree of vertical integration, geographical extent of markets served, nature of distribution channels employed, breadth of product line, etc. An industry, therefore, is composed of groups of firms, and firms in a group are similar to each other in terms of competitive strategy. An implication of the segmentation of industry into strategic groups is that the entry barriers are partly specific to the strategic groups and partly to the industry. The entry barriers not only impede fresh entry to the industry but also restrict the inter-strategic group mobility of the existing firms, and hence are more generally referred to as 'mobility barriers'. Thus, firms in a particular strategic group may enjoy protection not only from new entrants to the industry but also from existing firms belonging to other strategic groups in the same industry. The mobility barriers could be sources of persistent advantage, and hence might explain higher-profit firms in an industry. Porter (1979) used the hypothesis to explain the profit differences between 'leader' and 'follower' firms within US industries.

Kumar (1990b) used the mobility barriers hypothesis to explain the systematic differences observed between profit margins of MNE affiliates and local firms in forty-three Indian industries. He contended that MNE affiliates and local firms in host developing countries constituted two different strategic groups. Strategic differences between firms reflect their tangible and intangible assets. Being part of established global enterprises, MNE affiliates enjoy a dowry of intangible assets such as international brand names, proprietary technology, captive access to their parent's research laboratories, reservoirs of organizational and managerial skills, and international marketing and information networks. The determinants of profit margins of MNE affiliates and local firms were analysed across forty-three Indian industries to verify this contention. In the empirical tests the variables used for technology (both purchased and indigenously developed) and skill intensity turned out with positive and statistically significant coefficients in the case of MNE affiliates. In the case of profit functions of local firms, however, the coefficients of these variables were not significantly different from zero. The covariance analysis also confirmed the statistical significance of different slopes of the profit functions of MNE affiliates and their local counterparts. Therefore, technology and skill intensity act as mobility barriers protecting specific groups of firms, such as MNE affiliates, in developing countries. In other words, MNE affiliates enjoy a persistent source of market power in technology and skill-intensive industries because of their access to the technological resources of their parents.

The above discussion underlines the fact that technology has yet to receive due importance as an aspect of market structure and as an entry barrier in industry profitability studies. The situation is partly on account of data scarcity, measurement problems that in turn arise from the possibility of sourcing of technology from abroad, and partly from conceptual issues arising from strategic differences between industry firms that imply that technology intensity would be a source of market power for only some and not all industry firms. A limited number of studies that corrected for these problems did report the statistically significant effect of the technology factor.

TECHNOLOGY, COMPETITIVE RIVALRY AND CORPORATE PROFITS

The inter-firm variation in profitability within an industry has usually been explained in terms of market share or firm size and several aspects of the competitive conduct of firms, such as advertisement, R&D activity, vertical integration, product and geographical diversification, among other factors. Because R&D can be used by firms to obtain a competitive advantage over rivals with product improvements which are important sources of product differentiation, R&D intensity has been posited to have a favourable effect on a firm's profitability in much the same manner as advertisement intensity. The empirical verification of even this hypothesis has been affected by a number of problems. For one, R&D expenditures may have a lagged effect on a firm's performance. Hence, the current R&D expenditure may not be an appropriate measurement. Furthermore, R&D expenditure could be treated as an investment as it accumulates over time and generates a stream of lagged returns like fixed capital stock. Second, the relationship between R&D activity and profitability may be subject to simultaneity problem, as firms may invest their excess profits in R&D activity. Finally, as noted earlier, R&D may represent only a partial source of technological inputs for the firms, especially in developing countries where firms rely substantially on technology purchases from abroad.

The studies that took into account the problems involved in the empirical evaluation of the role of R&D or technological activities of firms in explaining their profits by appropriate methodological improvements found a statistically significant relationship. Grabowski and Mueller (1978) treated R&D as a capital cost rather than as a current expenditure, and found it to be an important determinant of profitability for US firms. Branch (1974) analysed the lagged R&D expenditure and profitability relationship for 111 large US firms in seven technology-intensive industries in the period 1950–65 in the framework of a simultaneous equation model. He found a significant effect of lagged R&D expenditure on current profitability in all seven industries. The lagged effect of profitability was also significant in determining current R&D expenditures in four industries. Connolly and Hirschey (1984) also corrected for the simultaneity bias while examining the relationship between R&D expenditure and a market value-based measure of profit margins for a sample of 390 of the *Fortune* 500 firms, and reported 'a regular and substantial positive simple effect' of R&D intensity on profitability (Connolly and Hirschey, 1984: 686). Profitability also increased R&D intensity.

As expenditures on technology purchase and import of capital goods are many times more than that on R&D in developing countries, some attempts have been made to take into account expenditures on technology other than R&D. Siddharthan (1988) considered two categories of technology expenditures in a study of Indian firms covering both privately held as well as publicly quoted companies. These were: import of capital goods; and R&D expenditures. The two groups of firms were considered as constituting different strategic groups, as the latter group generally included larger firms having access to the capital market for their expansion compared to the former. Although the import of capital goods favourably influenced the growth of sales for both types of firms, it influenced the profit margins differently. Capital goods imports improved the profit margins of the widely held companies but not the privately held ones. One possible reason for this differential behaviour could be the presence of size advantages in importing machinery which favour the larger firms. In both cases the levels of R&D expenditures did not contribute to profit margins, but percentage changes in the R&D expenditure favourably affected the growth of profits. These results, therefore, suggest that R&D activity has long-term implications for growth and not necessarily for short-run or immediate profit margins.

Siddharthan *et al.* (1994) analysed the inter-firm variations in performance for the top 385 private corporate firms in India in the framework of an econometric model developed to explain growth, profit margins, investments and financial choice of the firms. The technology variables considered included technology purchases from abroad against royalties, or lump sum and technical fee payments, and foreign equity participation. In addition, certain other variables incorporated were technology outputs such as royalty, lump sum and technical fee receipts; awards won for their R&D activities, and patents registered. Both the technology transfer variables, namely, foreign equity participation (intra-firm technology transfer) and technology imports through the market, had a significant and favourable influence on profit margins, but their influence on growth of sales was not significant. In India until recently, existing firms used technology imports mainly for the modernization of their plants and not for diversification into other activities. This was because firms had to obtain from the government a separate industrial approval or licence for diversification into new activities. The procedure to obtain an industrial licence to produce a new product for an existing firm was complex and time-consuming. For firms with substantial foreign equity participation the procedures were even more complex. Investments by MNEs were highly regulated and restricted, hence foreign equity participation was not an advantage for growth under the policy regime of the early 1980s (Kumar, 1994b: Chapter 1). On the other hand, diversification and growth were possible through in-house R&D. In fact, the policy encouraged the commercialization of R&D results. Hence technology receipts, the variable denoting technology output, was important in explaining growth of sales and not profit margins. The other two variables indicating R&D output, awards won from the government and the number of patents, were not useful in explaining either profit margins or growth. While the value of technology receipts is based on market evaluation, the other two variables are based on subjective evaluations, and this could be one of the reasons for their turning out not to be significant. While the policy regime in India prior to 1985 did not permit firms to take advantage of technological opportunities created abroad, the reforms introduced since 1985 permitted for the first time Indian firms to expand their product range, introduce new technologies, and increase their capacities without obtaining prior official sanction. This resulted in a noticeable increase in investment activities across Indian industries. A study by Pandit and Siddharthan (1997) based on the post-1985 dataset highlights the role of technology acquisition (in-house R&D, arm's-length purchase of technology, and intra-firm transfer of technology) in explaining inter-firm differences in the growth of capital stock. The study develops a theoretical model to consider the role of technology in stimulating investment, and presents the maximum likelihood estimates of the investment function for seven Indian industries for a sample consisting of 325 large corporate firms.

Some studies examined the implication of technological activity for profitability of R&D performing firms by computing the rate of return to investments in R&D. This stream of literature pioneered by Griliches has generally involved computing the R&D capital of firms with accumulated investments in R&D and introducing this variable as a factor of production, along with labour and fixed capital, in a production function. These studies have generally reported high rates of return to R&D capital, ranging between 9 and 69 per cent. In view of the existence of a recent and exhaustive survey of this stream of literature (see Griliches, 1995), these studies are not reviewed here. One recent study by Megna and Mueller (1991) examined the role of intangible capital created by past investments in R&D and advertising in explaining inter-firm differences in profits. Their results show significant differences in the returns to intangible capital across firms within each industry, even after controlling for firm-size and risk. The fact that intangible capital, unlike physical capital, cannot be purchased in competitive markets perhaps explains the persistence of intra-industry differences in profits.

Two recent attempts in this direction have been made in a developing country context. These are by Basant and Fikkert (1993) and Haksar (1995), both for India, and both using firm-level data produced by the country's central bank. Both studies report a substantial rate of return on R&D activity as well as on technology purchases from abroad. Raut (1995), for a sample of 192 Indian firms for the period 1975–86, found that spillover of others' R&D is a highly significant determinant of productivity growth in all industries except petro-chemicals. These studies are reviewed at a greater length in the context of spillovers of R&D as well as technology purchases from abroad (see Chapter 9).

TECHNOLOGICAL ACTIVITIES, PROFITABILITY AND CORPORATE GROWTH

Studies relating innovative activities to a firm's growth and profits are of a relatively recent origin. The neo-classical economic theory did not have a theory of the growth of firms. Neo-classical economists were primarily interested in maximizing profits, given the demand and cost structures. They were not concerned with the creation of new structures or with altering and shifting the demand and cost functions. The main purpose of innovative activity is to change the structures. Marris (1964) was the first to develop a rigorous model to analyse the growth and profits of firms. He posited growth of demand and growth of supply functions and determined the growth and profit margins using a set of equations. In his model he introduced the concept of the super environment in which a firm operates. This super environment could be influenced by technology expenditure which will enable a firm to shift its growth–profit frontier in such a way that the firm enjoys both higher growth and higher profits simultaneously. In the absence of changing the super environment, however, pursuit of higher growth beyond a point would entail a sacrifice of profits at the margin. Despite the fact that the work was published in 1964, the impact of technological expenditure in shifting the growth–profit frontier was not investigated empirically till the early 1980s.

Siddharthan and Lall (1982) analysed the growth and profit behaviour of the top seventy-four US MNCs for the period 1976–9 in the Marris framework. They introduced R&D, expenditures on product differentiation and multinationality as variables that are likely to shift the growth–profit frontier. Their results highlighted the role of R&D in fostering the growth of these MNCs. R&D expenditures promoted growth for firms producing both consumer and producer goods, while advertisement expenditures aided growth only for the firms producing non-consumer goods. Their results further demonstrated that informational advertising, especially when backed by genuine product differentiation based on R&D, was conducive to growth, while persuasive advertising that was not backed by R&D merely diverted resources away from growth into wasteful competition. Therefore, R&D occupied a prominent position in elevating a firm's performance.

Hall (1987) used a panel data for the period 1976–83 on publicly traded US manufacturing firms and analysed, among other things, the impact of R&D on two variables: the probability of a firm's survival; and growth rate. Regarding a firm's survival, his results showed that firms with a larger portion of their assets in R&D are less likely to disappear from the sample. While analysing growth rate, he compared the relative importance of physical investments and R&D. His results showed that an increase of four million dollars in physical investment was associated with 1 per cent increase in annual growth rate, while only two million dollars of R&D investment achieved the same purpose. Furthermore, his finding that R&D expenditure was a more important predictor of growth than expenditures on physical capital was robust across size classes.

Another theory that related the growth of firms to technology is the product lifecycle theory that linked firm growth with the introduction of new products, product diversification and innovation. The argument runs as follows: all firms would like their growth curves to be exponential so that they grow at a compound rate. On the other hand the sales curve of a product is not exponential but is 'S'-shaped or logistic, characterized by three stages, the first denoted by high technological change but very low growth rate, the second indicated by very high growth rate and stabilizing technology, and the third by declining growth or even negative growth resulting in an actual fall in sales and the standardization of technology. Given the shape of the product lifecycles, it was not possible to grow at an exponential rate by producing and selling the same product, as all products will touch the third stage of their sales curve, namely, the declining part of the curve, sooner or later. Under these conditions, continuing high growth in the overall sales of a firm is possible only through product diversification and differentiation. In other words, firms should produce a large number of products that are in different stages of their lifecycles: some in the first – the products just created through R&D; some in the second stage – the stage of high growth; and the rest in the third stage. Here, when the high-growth products reach the third stage, there should be enough products passing through the first stage to occupy the vacant second stage. This in turn would imply that a firm should be doing enough R&D to introduce new products continuously. Thus, without continuous R&D, enduring growth is not possible. Furthermore, not all newly created products need be successful commercially. Some of the new products might not attain the high-growth stage at all. This enhances the role of R&D and underlines the need to introduce new products on a continuing basis.

CONCLUDING REMARKS AND POLICY IMPLICATIONS

This chapter has discussed the treatment in the theoretical and empirical literature of the role that technological activities play in determining industry and firm profitability and growth. The early empirical studies suffered from a number of measurement, specification and conceptual problems that prevented a fuller appreciation of the role that technology plays in shaping the inter-industry and inter-firm patterns of profitability. More recent studies that took care of these problems have statistically verified an important role played by technology and the technological activities of firms in determining their profitability as an entry barrier and as an important aspect of conduct. Studies have also highlighted the accumulative and investment-like nature of technological activities and have estimated high rates of return on the intangible capital created by the stream of R&D expenditure. The technological activities of firms have also been found to play an important role in determining the growth rate of firms. Corporate growth is translated into national growth rates, and hence the technological activities of national firms contribute to the growth of national economies.

The obvious implication of these findings of the literature is that firm-level technological activities need to be encouraged in developing countries. Despite the high rates of return reported by most of the studies that computed them, developing country firms may not be willing to invest in R&D activity on their own initiative because of, among other factors, the highly risky nature of such activity, the firms' smaller size and hence their inability to invest in the necessary infrastructure for undertaking R&D, and the lack of skills, financing, etc. Government policy, therefore, can play an important role in promoting firm-level R&D activities by providing finance and sharing the R&D costs and hence the risks, by creating the institutional infrastructure such as tool-rooms and other common facility centres so that individual firms could draw upon them, by encouraging industry associations to undertake R&D on common industry problems, by the formation of R&D consortia among national firms, by expanding technical education facilities to ensure an adequate supply of R&D personnel, and through various other direct and indirect policy instruments. The propensity of national firms to undertake R&D may to some extent also be determined by the nature and extent of technology imports. This will be discussed in Chapter 9.

Part III

TECHNOLOGY, TRADE AND MULTINATIONAL ENTERPRISES

The external economic linkages of enterprises, i.e. international trade, foreign technology purchases, and affiliation with multinational enterprises, have important implications for their technological effort. The causality is hardly of a one-way nature in that the technological effort of enterprises may determine their overseas linkages, and especially their trade. With increasing liberalization and economic integration of the world economy, these linkages have assumed greater importance than ever. The focus of this part is on the interaction of the technological effort of enterprises with their external linkages of different forms. Chapter 7 discusses the implications of having a controlling stake of multinational enterprises or foreign direct investment on the conduct of local firms, and other related issues. Chapter 8 discusses the issues concerning the relationship between the technological effort of enterprises and their international trade. Finally, Chapter 9 discusses the implications of technology purchases from abroad on the building of domestic technological capability in the host country.

7

MULTINATIONAL ENTERPRISES, TECHNOLOGY AND MARKET STRUCTURE

INTRODUCTION

As indicated in Chapter 1, multinational enterprises (MNEs) dominate the world's pool of technology, controlling between 80 and 85 per cent of global patents. MNEs also account for much of the technology transfers, either through the package of foreign direct investments (FDI) or through licensing and other contractual arrangements that have evolved over time. Technology and the creation of other firm-specific knowledge that affects market structure and firm performance, as seen in the previous chapter, also play a central role in the evolution of national firms into international or multinational enterprises in the theory, and hence in the explanation, of FDI. Furthermore, FDI is not only a channel of technology transfer, for the foreign ownership and bundle of intangible assets that accompany it affect the firm's conduct in a significant manner. Hence, it is also considered as an element of market structure in open economy models of competition (see, for instance, Caves *et al.*, 1980).

This chapter highlights the interaction between technology, market structure and the foreign ownership of industries. The next section summarizes the contemporary theory of international operations of the firm and the empirical evidence on determinants of FDI and technology licensing. The following section discusses the theoretical and empirical issues concerned with the impact of MNE operations on host country market structures. The chapter then goes on to review the recent advances in industrial organization theory that recognize the intra-industry strategic differences. It summarizes recent empirical work that extends these concepts to analyse the implications of MNE affiliates' ownership of knowledge and other intangible assets, and the resulting strategic differences on their relative performance. After that, an important development in the field of international business over the past fifteen years is briefly examined, i.e. the evolution of outward FDI flows from developing countries. Topics include the motives, significance and patterns of internationalization of developing country enterprises and their implications. The final section concludes the chapter with a summary of policy implications.

DETERMINANTS OF MNE ACTIVITY ABROAD: THEORY AND EMPIRICAL EVIDENCE

Theory of international operations of firms

FDI is generally associated with large corporations with international operations called transnational or multinational enterprises (MNEs). Economic theory has dealt with FDI (and licensing) in the context of an explanation for the internationalization of firms. In fact exporting, FDI and licensing of technology are treated in theory as alternative means of operating abroad.

Hymer (1960, published 1976) made a first systematic attempt to explain the internationalization of firms. Before that, FDI flows were treated like any other international flows of resources such as portfolio investments and were thought to be driven by international factor price differentials. Since Hymer's contribution, the theory has evolved with the contributions of Vernon (1966), Kindleberger (1969), Caves (1971, 1974a, 1996), Buckley and Casson (1976), Dunning (1979, 1981), Rugman (1981), Teece (1981, 1983), Williamson (1981), and Hennart (1982), among others. Dunning has drawn upon different approaches in his 'eclectic theory' in an attempt to provide a comprehensive and general explanation of different types of international operations.

The extent and mode of overseas expansion of a firm is determined by three factors in the eclectic theory: ownership advantages, locational advantages, and internalization incentives. A firm wishing to operate abroad must possess advantages sufficient to more than offset the handicaps faced in an alien atmosphere and to cover the greater risks (Hymer, 1960; Kindleberger, 1969; Caves, 1971). These advantages emanate from the ownership of the proprietary intangible assets possessed by firms which can be productively employed abroad. These assets could include, among others: brand goodwill, technology (patented and otherwise), managerial and marketing skills, and access to cheaper sources of capital and raw materials. Initially (in the first phase of the product cycle, according to Vernon, 1966) these advantages are exploited abroad through exports from the home base of the firm. In the subsequent stages, production is moved closer to the export markets with FDI, because locational advantages, which make it more profitable than exports, begin to emerge. These advantages arise from factors such as tariffs and quantitative restrictions imposed on imports by host countries, communication and transport costs, and inter-country differences in input/factor prices and productivity.

Due to imperfections in the market for knowledge and other intangible assets, ownership and locational advantages usually provided sufficient conditions for FDI flows during the early post-war period. In the period following the late 1960s, however, the standardization of a wide variety of technologies, and hence the increasing competition coupled with the improved bargaining position of host country governments, provided arm's-length licensing of intangible assets as an alternative to FDI (Dunning, 1983). Mere ownership of intangible assets and the presence of locational advantages were no longer sufficient, though still necessary, conditions for FDI. These advantages needed to be complemented by some incentives for internalization of the markets of intangible assets and hence result in transfer on an intra-firm basis or through FDI (Buckley and Casson, 1976; Dunning, 1979; Rugman, 1981; Williamson, 1981; Caves, 1996; Hennart, 1982). The internalization incentives could arise because of market failures and information asymmetry involved in their transfer. The (external) markets for intangible assets are often inefficient channels for their transfer because of a number of infirmities which emanate from the characteristics of intangible assets. First, because of their 'public goods'-like nature, the marginal cost of their use elsewhere is close to zero. Hence, they are inefficiently priced. Second, a severe information asymmetry exists which results from the inability of the seller to make a convincing disclosure about the intangible asset. This is particularly applicable in the case of unpatented process know-how. Third, the unaffiliated firms abroad may fail to recognize the productive potential of technological developments taking place in a country. Fourth, there may be the buyer's uncertainty about the claims of the supplier regarding the potential value of the intangible asset. Fifth, there may be problems with codification of knowledge. Certain kinds of knowledge may be embodied in the skills of personnel or may have a high tacit component, hence their transfer will not be complete without physical transfer of personnel. Finally, the arm's-length market may fail to ensure uniform quality standards which are important, particularly in the case of the transfer of goodwill assets like brand names.

These infirmities lead to a high cost of market transactions (transaction or governance costs) of intangible assets. Firms tend to avoid these costs by internalizing the transactions of the intangible assets or by undertaking FDI. However, there may be certain costs associated with internalization itself. Coordination of manufacturing units located in geographical areas separated by national boundaries entails certain information costs. Further, the host country government may discriminate against enterprises under foreign control and hence there may be certain political costs. In addition, there are the administration costs of internal markets depending upon the degree of professionalization of management. Therefore, firms weigh the economies arising from the internalization of a transaction and the costs associated with it. Firms prefer to internalize a transaction (or undertake FDI) if the transaction cost economies outweigh the additional costs of internalization. Otherwise the intangible assets are licensed to unaffiliated firms abroad through the markets. Thus the presence of internalization incentives provides the final requirement for the explanation of FDI.

Besides the characteristics of intangible assets or technology to be transferred as predicted by the theory, a number of other factors may in practice affect the choice between FDI and licensing. For instance, licensing is preferred when FDI is not profitable or possible. This could be because of the small size of the market, or government restrictions on FDI. Licensing is encouraged when the licenser lacks experience in managing manufacturing plants abroad. Licensing may also be preferred when an industry's technology is changing rapidly, because the lead time required to license an established producer is usually less than that required to start a subsidiary from scratch (Davidson and McFetridge, 1985; Caves, 1996).

The implications of the theory are that exporting and foreign production through either licensing or FDI are alternative modes of overseas operations. In the absence of any restrictions on imports and factor price differences, firms wishing to serve a particular market will rely on exports. Seen this way, excessive trade liberalization may erode the locational advantage of a country as a location of production for the local market, and lead to deindustrialization. MNEs may prefer to export to the country from some other plants and their local operations may be reduced to assembling, packaging, marketing and after-sales service-type operations. A number of empirical studies have confirmed the interdependence of exporting and FDI (or foreign production) (see, for instance, Hirsch, 1976; Baldwin, 1979; Lall, 1980a; Buckley and Pearce, 1981). The choice of the mode of foreign production is determined by the transaction costs involved in market transfer, which would be determined by the nature of intangible assets. Process technologies which are covered by intellectual property rights such as patents, and which can be codified in the form of designs and drawings, can be transferred easily on a licensing basis. Transfer of product technologies, especially the branded ones and process technologies not covered by patents, or those with a high content of idiosyncratic inputs, are subject to greater transaction costs. Hence, FDI will generally be a predominant mode for transfer in these cases.

Empirical analysis of the determinants of FDI

The determinants of FDI have been analysed at either inter-country, inter-industry, or inter-temporal levels. The inter-country studies explain the pattern of FDI inflows across countries in terms of country characteristics. Basically these studies analyse the locational factors in determining the country choice in the FDI decision-making of MNEs. These studies may be useful in the formulation of an FDI promotion policy. The inter-industry studies analyse variations in the intensity of FDI outflows across industries from a particular country, or inter-industry variations in the intensity of FDI inflows in a particular country. These studies help in understanding the characteristics of industries that could attract FDI and/or licensed technologies. Finally, inter-temporal studies explain variations in FDI inflows in a country over time in terms of policy changes and macro-economic performance variables. These studies may help in the evaluation of the efficacy of a particular set of policies and for formulating strategies to promote FDI inflows.

In view of the fact that the empirical studies of the determinants of FDI have recently been extensively surveyed by UNCTC (1992) and Dunning (1993: chapter 6), we confine ourselves to a rather selective and brief review of the findings of a few recent studies.

Inter-country studies

Among the inter-country studies, Root and Ahmed (1979), Kudrle (1984), Schneider and Frey (1985), Contractor (1990), Balasubramanyam and Salisu (1991), Agarwal *et al.* (1991), Koechlin (1992), Wheeler and Mody (1992), and Moore (1993) have analysed the determinants of FDI flows from a particular country or from all OECD countries to different samples of countries. Despite the divergent samples, measurements of variables, and methodologies used by these studies, there is a broad convergence in their findings. Among the factors that favoured FDI inflows are the level of prosperity as measured by the *per capita* income, market size in terms of national income, growth rates, extent of industrialization and urbanization and the quality of infrastructure available. High rates of inflation, current account deficits and political instability adversely affected the prospects for FDI inflow. In addition, the number of man-days lost in strikes, etc., representing the quality of industrial relations, was found to have a significant negative impact in the case of FDI in the Asian and Pacific developing countries by Rana (1988), who found the credit rating of a country also to be a significant positive determinant of FDI inflows. Geographical distance, language, the economic/political and military dependence of a potential host on the source country, labour cost and business environment risk index were also found to be significant factors in determining US FDI flows between 1966 and 1985 by Koechlin.

Policy factors such as the degree of openness of an economy, incentives and tax rates, etc., have generally not proved to be significant determinants of FDI inflows. Contractor (1990) in his empirical study of forty-six countries did not find liberalization to be an important factor in influencing the pattern of FDI flows. The foreign investors' response was found to be strongly influenced by the size and growth of the host economy rather than by changes in the government's FDI policies. Wheeler and Mody (1992), in their study covering forty-two countries for the period 1982 to 1988, emphasized the importance of the quality of infrastructure, the level of industrialization and market size in attracting US FDI. Open market policies or incentives such as tax breaks were found to be of limited value in determining the investment decisions of US MNEs. In a recent paper, Loree and Guisinger (1995) found some support for incentives in influencing the inter-country pattern of US FDI outflows. Yet they found no evidence to suggest that 'a dollar spent on incentives has a higher return, in the form of investment attracted, than a dollar spent on infrastructure'. Agarwal *et al.* (1991: 128), finding the irrelevance of specific incentives and attractions offered to foreign investors, concluded that what is good policy for domestic investors – for instance, a stable and favourable general framework for investment – is also good for foreign investors.

The role of intellectual property protection in influencing FDI flows has also been debated. Bosworth (1980) and Frischtak (1989) did not find a significant role of IPRs in influencing the pattern of FDI and technology transfers respectively. Ferrantino (1993) found no discernible impact of a country's adherence to IPR agreements on arm's-length exports or subsidiary sales (i.e. FDI) of US firms. But subsidiaries in countries adhering to IPRs had a greater chance of sourcing more components from the US than from host countries. The affiliates in countries belonging to the Paris Convention are also likely to have higher payments of royalties and licence fees than others. Greater dependence on parents for sourcing components also creates greater potential for transfer pricing. Since the 'US is generally a low tax regime compared to LDCs, this suggests that strong international IPRs may indirectly cause a diversion of tax revenue from LDCs to the US treasury' (Ferrantino 1993: 329). Kondo (1994), in a Harvard University PhD dissertation, found no consistently significant relationship between the strength of patent laws in terms of four alternative indicators and the levels of and changes in US FDI in a sample of thirty-three countries over a fifteen-year period. Mansfield (1994), on the other hand, cites some tentative unpublished results of research undertaken by Lee which suggest that the weakness of intellectual property protection as perceived by firms adversely affected US capital outflow in a sample of sixteen countries if the size of the country was held constant, Japan was excluded, and Mexico was separated with a dummy variable. These results, however, are at best conjectural because of specification errors, subjective bias in the measurement of IPRs, and the small sample of countries. Mansfield himself cautions about inferring too much from them. Kumar (1996b) found the strength of the IPR regime of host countries unable to explain the R&D investments of US MNEs while analysing their determinants across countries. However, the strength of IPRs could influence the nature or direction of R&D investments. Clearly, there is need for a more rigorous analysis of the role of IPRs in influencing the magnitudes and composition of FDI.

Finally, Kumar (1994a) has found export-oriented FDIs to be of a special type, even more unevenly concentrated than local market-oriented FDIs. Apparently MNEs are more selective while choosing a location for export-oriented production. These investments have depended on the availability of low-cost labour and natural resources as expected, and also on industrial capability and the presence of export processing zones giving them freedom from the trade regimes of the host countries. The other aspects of host country policies and the overall international orientation of the economy were found to be insignificant factors in explaining the attractiveness of a country for such investments.

The implications from the body of literature for the determinants of FDI inflows, as reviewed above, is that low-income, agrarian economies with relatively poor availability of infrastructure have a limited scope for attracting FDI inflows. The liberalization of policy regimes, investment incentives and strengthening of intellectual property rights may be of limited help, if at all. This is clear from the recent trends of declining shares in global inflows of FDI of low-income countries such as those in South Asia and sub-Saharan Africa despite the liberalization of their investment and trade regimes. The bulk of FDI inflows to developing countries continues to be concentrated in a handful of middle-income countries in East and Southeast Asia and Latin America. China has been highly successful in attracting large magnitudes of FDI in recent years, despite its low *per capita* income. But FDI in China is of a very special type. The bulk of FDI in China is by the non-resident Chinese based in Hong Kong, Taiwan, Macao, Singapore, rather than by the Western MNEs which are targeted by most developing countries. Finally, competition for attracting export-oriented FDIs is even keener among developing countries, and the MNEs pick up the winners.

Inter-industry studies

Inter-industry studies have either explained variation across industries in outward FDIs from a home country or shares of inward FDIs in a host country. Pugel (1978), Lall (1980a), Bergsten *et al.* (1978) and Denekamp (1995) explained inter-industry variation of US outward FDI, and Swedenborg (1979) that of Swedish outward FDI. Caves (1974a), Caves *et al.* (1980), Saunders (1982) and Owen (1982) have explained variation in foreign shares across Canadian industries, Lall and Siddharthan (1982) have done the same for the USA, and Lall and Mohammed (1983a) and Kumar (1987c) for Indian industries. Most of the studies have ignored the possibility of arm's-length licensing as an alternative and have concentrated on FDI. The main findings of these studies include FDI intensity varying positively with advertisement intensity, skill intensity, R&D intensity and capital requirement intensity of the industry, among other factors.

Kumar (1987c) considered the FDI versus licensing choice, and analysed determinants of their intensity across forty-nine Indian manufacturing industries for the period 1980–1. He found FDI to be concentrated in advertising and human skill-intensive industries and licensing in industries where know-how could be embodied in plant and machinery, or those with less complex machinery. Neither FDI nor licensing was concentrated in the large capital-requiring industries, apparently because of the development of local capital markets and term lending institutions. The import substitution industrialization strategy prompted the erstwhile exporters to the country to set up manufacturing plants in the country. Host country protection was also found to be important in explaining FDI in US industries by Lall and Siddharthan (1982). The host country protection granted to local industries acts as a locational factor prompting exporters to set up local production to retain their markets in the countries.

Kumar (1990d) found US MNEs to prefer FDI for transfer of product technologies, and licensing for transfer of process technologies. Kumar (1995a) has highlighted the fact that the selective policy that the Indian government followed over the 1970s and early 1980s favoured licensing as a mode of local production in India and affected the balance between FDI and licensing in the country.

The implication of the above literature is that, in the absence of any policy factors, the choice between FDI and licensing will be determined by the transaction costs. Since transaction costs are quite significant for branded consumer goods, much of the FDI will be concentrated in those industries. Thus liberalization of policy should make the effect of intangible assets and internalization incentives more pronounced. This is a hypothesis for future research.

Inter-temporal studies

Inter-temporal studies have explained variations in FDI inflows in a country over time in terms of policy changes and macro-economic performance variables. Examples of this stream of literature include Riedel (1975) and Tsai (1991) for Taiwan, Agarwal (1990) for eight Pacific Rim countries; Lucas (1993) for East and Southeast Asian countries; and UNCTAD (1993) for different regions. Of these, Lucas's study is the most interesting from the policy perspective, as he attempted to capture the effect of prices and wages on FDI inflows, and so is singled out for a comment. He estimates a model of derived demand for foreign capital for a profit maximizing multiple product monopolist for seven countries in Southeast and East Asia, i.e. Indonesia, Korea, Malaysia, the Philippines, Singapore, Taiwan and Thailand for the period 1961–87. FDI inflow at constant prices (deflated by deflator for fixed capital formation) and net of depreciation is found to be responsive to cost and prices for all countries with the exception of Taiwan. FDI inflows are less elastic to a rise in capital costs than to a rise in wages. Domestic investment affects foreign inflow favourably in Korea, Malaysia, Singapore and the Philippines (a weak relationship); inversely in Indonesia; and has no clear relationship in Taiwan and Thailand. A higher risk of currency depreciation captured in terms of months of imports covered by foreign exchange reserves discourages FDI inflows. A greater incidence of industrial disputes also deters FDI. An enhanced size of domestic and export markets (the latter represented by the GDP of major export markets) favours FDI inflows. The elasticity with respect to export markets is greater than that for domestic market size. Lucas infers from this that inward orientation may not be a necessary condition for attracting FDI. This finding, however, could not be generalized, because the sample comprises countries that have all pursued export-oriented strategies. It remains to be seen if the same holds good for an economy, such as India, with a large domestic market. Finally, the study brings out the role of influential episodes in a country's history in affecting the FDI inflows, for example the Asian games in Korea, Aquino's succession in the Philippines, and the US build-up in Thailand brought in more FDI, while Sukarno's rule in Indonesia, Park's assassination in Korea, and Marcos's martial law in the Philippines reduced it.

MNEs AND MARKET STRUCTURE, CONDUCT AND PERFORMANCE (S–C–P) IN HOST COUNTRIES

The studies analysing the impact of MNEs or FDI on host country market structures, conduct and performance have confined themselves to an examination of relationships between FDI and the level of concentration, advertisement and R&D intensities or performance in terms of profitability. Lall (1978a) provides an early survey of the literature; see Caves (1996) for a more recent survey.

Univariate comparisons

Market structure can be affected by the relative scale of operation of enterprises. A number of studies have provided evidence on the larger scale of operations of foreign enterprises than that of their local counterparts; for instance, Newfarmer and Mueller (1975) for Mexico and Brazil; Lall and Streeten (1977) for India, Colombia and Malaysia. Radhu (1973) in Pakistan, and Willmore (1976) in Guatemala, have observed significant correlation between the degree of the presence of MNEs and seller concentration. Evans (1977) and Willmore (1989) for Brazil, Lall (1979) for Malaysia, and Blomström (1986) for Mexico, found a positive influence of foreign ownership on industry concentration, even after controlling for entry barriers.

Conduct has been compared in terms of advertising and R&D behaviour. Caves *et al.* (1980) and Gupta (1983) found the foreign share in industry sales to have a significant positive influence in explaining the proportion of advertising expenditure in Canadian manufacturing industries. This could be due to two reasons: foreign subsidiaries spend a relatively higher proportion of their income on advertising, so that the industry average of advertising expenditure rises in proportion to their presence; and foreign subsidiaries induce the industry to pursue a non-price rivalry, and both foreign and local firms spend a higher proportion of income on advertising. Which of the two effects is dominant, however, is not clear from the two studies. Willmore (1986) found foreign enterprises to spend a higher proportion of sales on advertising than their local counterparts in Brazil, even after controlling for firm size and industry. Fairchild and Sosin (1986) and Kumar (1987b) reported that local firms had a greater inclination to undertake in-house R&D activity than their foreign controlled counterparts. Lall (1985: chapter 7) found a positive relationship between foreign ownership and R&D in the Indian engineering industry, but a negative one in the chemical industry. Braga and Willmore (1991) found a positive effect of foreign ownership on the probability of firms having a systematic programme of new product development in the Brazilian industry.

MNE affiliates or foreign owned firms can be expected to enjoy higher profitability than their local counterparts because of their monopolistic ownership of intangible assets, and the prices charged by them may include monopoly rents for goodwill and other intangible assets held. The evidence from the literature gives the impression that MNE affiliates fare better than local firms in terms of profitability. However, the observed differences did not prevail when extraneous factors were controlled for. Examples include Lall (1976) for Colombia and India, Gershenberg and Ryan (1978) for Uganda, and Fairchild and Sosin (1986) for the Latin American countries. Subrahmanian (1972), Fairchild (1977), Newfarmer and Marsh (1981) and Ahiakpor (1986a) also did not find any significant difference between the profitability of MNE affiliates and their local counterparts in Indian, Mexican, Brazilian, and Ghanian case studies, respectively. Reported profits, however, need not necessarily reflect true profits, since they are subject to possible manipulations such as transfer pricing.

Towards a framework for comparisons: rivalry and strategic groups

The above findings on behavioural differences between MNE affiliates and their local counterparts, however, have not been woven into a coherent framework. Furthermore, extraneous factors have very seldom been controlled for, as most of these studies have been made in univariate frameworks. Kumar (1990a: chapter 4) noted the findings for univariate and multivariate tests of comparisons of foreign and local firms in India to be quite different. Kumar (1991) attempted to provide a framework explaining behavioural differences between foreign and local enterprises in a country. He contended that the basic difference between MNE affiliates and local firms is their mode of competitive rivalry. MNE affiliates enjoy a dowry of intangible assets, such as internationally recognized brand names, captive access to technology and reservoirs of technical, managerial and organizational skills. In order to maximize the revenue productivity of these assets, MNE affiliates are more likely to pursue non-price modes of rivalry than are their local counterparts. The choice of the mode of rivalry is reflected in different aspects of a firm's conduct and performance.

Non-price modes of rivalry are generally accompanied by extensive advertising and marketing campaigns to disseminate the differentiating features of their products among potential customers. Hence, MNE affiliates are expected to have a higher advertising intensity than their local counterparts. MNE affiliates are considered to favour larger scales of operations intended to serve the national markets because of the significant scale economies involved in advertisement activity. MNE affiliates are also expected to have a greater degree of vertical integration to avoid the risk of losing trade secrets in the course of the transfer of component designs and specifications to subcontractors and because of the reduced scope of subcontracting due to product specificity. MNE affiliates are expected to employ proportionately more highly skilled personnel and managers than local firms because product rivalry involves skill-intensive activities such as advertising, specialized marketing, quality control and product development. Besides brand names and advertising, the product is often differentiated by the superiority of the overall package offered in terms of generous credit terms, superior after-sales service and so on. MNEs can be expected to have a greater degree of liquidity in order to be able to extend the manufacturer's credits to dealers/buyers. Finally, the monopolistic environment that MNE affiliates create by product differentiation may allow them to earn super-normal profits. Hence, profit margins of MNEs may be higher than those of local firms.

The empirical findings of Kumar (1991) relating to a comparison of the behaviour of two groups of firms in forty-nine Indian industries in the framework of both univariate and multivariate discriminant techniques were in tune with the above predictions. They reveal that MNE affiliates operate at relatively larger scales, enjoy higher profit margins and are more vertically integrated, fund-flush firms that employ more skilled personnel. With regard to advertising and R&D, they also benefit from the global expenditures of their associates. The tendency of MNE affiliates to opt for non-price modes of rivalry has important implications for the market structure and competitive situation in the host developing countries. MNE affiliates' preference to operate on a larger scale and to depend more heavily on marketing, advertising and R&D activity to differentiate their products, raises barriers to the entry of new firms. These 'contrived barriers' to entry perhaps explain the continued domination by MNE affiliates of several brand-sensitive consumer goods industries, despite instruments of the Indian government's policy which sought to curb monopolies (Kumar, 1990a: chapter 2).

TECHNOLOGY, STRATEGIC GROUPS AND MOBILITY BARRIERS

If MNE affiliates do indeed enjoy a dowry of technology and other intangible assets and follow a different mode of rivalry from their local counterparts, as the literature reviewed in the previous section seems to suggest, they perhaps could be constituting different strategic groups within the same industries, of the type that Porter (1979) described (see pp. 80–2). Kumar (1990b) argued that MNE affiliates and local firms in India belonged to different strategic groups in view of the observed differences in their conduct, as reported earlier. In Porter's proposition, entry barriers become partly specific to strategic groups and partly to the industry. The entry barriers not only impede fresh entry to the industry but also restrict mobility between strategic groups for the existing firms, and hence are more generally referred to as 'mobility barriers'. Thus, firms in a particular strategic group may not only enjoy protection from new entrants to the industry but also from existing firms belonging to other strategic groups in the same industry.

If MNE affiliates and local firms indeed belonged to different strategic groups, the entry or mobility barrier variables, i.e. product differentiation, technology intensity and skill intensity, would affect their profit margins differently. MNE affiliates would be protected by mobility barriers not only from potential entrants to the industry but also from other existing industry firms. Therefore, an empirical verification of this contention was made by examining the determinants of profit margins of MNE affiliates and local firms in forty-three Indian manufacturing industries (see Kumar, 1990b). In the empirical tests, while for the variables capturing technology and skill intensity entry or mobility barriers turned out with positive and statistically significant coefficients in the case of MNE affiliates, they had coefficients not significantly different from zero in the case of local firms. The covariance analysis further confirmed the statistical significance of the differences in the slopes of the profit functions for the two groups of firms. Technology intensity in this exercise was measured in terms of both the firms' own technological effort and expenditure on technology purchase. It is interesting also to note that, in a restricted model estimated for the pooled sample containing observations from both groups where the intercept alone was allowed to vary across the groups, the technology variable was statistically insignificant.

Thus the empirical analysis finds support for the proposition that MNE affiliates and local firms constitute different strategic groups within specific industries, and that the former as a group enjoy greater protection from mobility barriers. MNEs appear to enjoy persistent advantages over their local counterparts, especially in knowledge-intensive (both technology and human skill) industries. This is because in such industries the overall technological strength and reputation of an enterprise and the width of the product and service range play a crucial role in market transactions. Being part of global enterprises, MNE affiliates enjoy a formidable edge over local firms in these respects. The two groups of firms seem to serve different market segments. MNE affiliates concentrate on the upper end of the market, consisting of discriminating consumers who can accept higher prices, and local firms on the usually more price-competitive lower end (Kumar, 1990a).

OUTWARD FOREIGN DIRECT INVESTMENT BY DEVELOPING COUNTRY ENTERPRISES

FDI flows have traditionally originated in industrialized countries. However, since the late 1970s, FDI outflows from some developing countries have taken place and have indeed grown rapidly. Developing country enterprises have increasingly used FDI abroad as a means of acquiring technology and market access, and for strengthening their international competitiveness through international rationalization of production. FDI made by developing country enterprises could be classified into four broad types according to motivations in a similar way to FDI originating in industrialized countries. Market-seeking FDI is undertaken to obviate trade barriers in the host countries. The initial round of FDI from developing countries was comprised mostly of market-seeking FDI made in other developing countries. Trade-supporting FDI is undertaken in major markets to create a marketing network and to provide aftersales services. Since international competitiveness is increasingly determined by non-price factors such as the ability to provide after-sales services, an increasing number of developing country enterprises have set up trade-supporting affiliates in the industrialized countries in the recent period to support their operations. Efficiency-seeking FDI is undertaken to exploit the availability of cheaper raw materials or factors of production in other countries. Exporters from East Asian newly industrializing economies, such as Korea, Taiwan and Hong Kong, that have been affected by rising domestic wages and currency appreciations, are increasingly relocating labour intensive production in neighbouring developing countries with cheap labour. Finally, some developing country enterprises have set up subsidiaries in major centres of knowledge creation in their fields to benefit from knowledge spillovers, e.g. investments made by Korean micro-electronic firms and Indian software companies in Silicon Valley (Kumar, 1995a,b). Sometimes developing country enterprises also engage themselves in acquisitions of established corporations in industrialized countries to gain access to technology, brand names, and markets, just as do MNEs from industrialized countries. These could be classified as strategic asset-seeking FDIs.

FDI flows originating in developing countries have evolved over time not only in terms of increasing magnitudes but also in terms of their motivations. In the initial round, developing country FDI outflows were generally destined for other developing countries, seeking markets, and essentially horizontal in nature. Since the mid-1980s, FDI flows from developing countries have grown rapidly into sizeable magnitudes (see Table 7.1). It has been argued that this period also marks the beginning of a change in motivation of these flows (Kumar, 1995b). Developing country enterprises have increasingly used FDI as a strategic tool for promoting their competitiveness abroad in the more recent period. This transformation has been prompted by the recent global trend of the emergence of regional trading blocs and rising protectionist tendencies in industrialized countries. Besides, the international competitiveness of a few East Asian newly industrializing economies, e.g. South Korea, Hong Kong and Taiwan, has been affected by currency appreciation, rising domestic wages and the exhaustion of MFA quotas. Enterprises from affected countries have responded by moving production abroad to maintain their international competitiveness. The developing country governments have also recognized the strategic role of outward FDI in strengthening competitiveness abroad by liberalizing policy regimes, as well as providing financial and other incentives (see Kumar, 1995c, for more details).

An indication of the change in motivation of developing country FDIs since the mid-1980s is given by their changing geographical distribution. Table 7.2 shows the increasing concentration of FDI from developing countries in the industrialized countries. The early outflows of FDI from developing countries had been concentrated among developing countries, as is clear from the rather small share of industrialized countries in outward FDI stock for most of the developing home countries. The increasing concentration of developing country FDI in industrialized countries which are principal markets for their goods in the more recent period tends to suggest an increasing orientation of these investments towards strengthening international competitiveness from their market-seeking nature in the early years.

The increasing attention paid by developing country enterprises to industrialized countries over the years, however, does not diminish the importance of these enterprises as sources of FDI for developing countries. Except for a couple of countries, the bulk of FDI from developing countries is still

Table 7.1 Stock of outward FDIs made by select Asian countries, 1980–93 (US$ million)

Country	1980	1985	1990	1993
South Korea	142	487	2172	5632
Taiwan	101	215	3075	5619*
Hong Kong	1800	9441	18930	n.a.
Singapore	652	1320	4277	6236
China	39	131	2488	7402*
India	149	180	290	707

* belongs to 1992
Source: Kumar (1995c)

Table 7.2 Industrialized countries' share in outward FDI stock of developing countries

Home Country	Industrialized countries' share	
	1980	*1991*
China	34	71
Hong Kong	8	18
India	11	19
Singapore	9	21
South Korea	32	56

Source: Kumar (1995c)

concentrated in other developing countries. Despite their relatively small overall magnitude, FDI inflows originating in developing countries hold an important place in a number of developing countries. Kumar (1995b) has shown that FDI flows from developing countries accounted for 65 per cent of inward FDI stock in China in 1990, nearly 50 per cent in Sri Lanka, 41 per cent in Malaysia, 37 per cent in Paraguay, and was approaching 30 per cent in Indonesia, Chile and Taiwan. The East Asian developing countries were responsible for 50.6 per cent of all FDI approvals in 1990–1 in Indonesia and 44.6 and 25.6 per cent of FDI approvals in Thailand in 1990 and 1991 respectively (Wells, 1993). Furthermore, 46 per cent of all FDI projects originating in East Asian countries approved in Indonesia between 1990 and 1991 were of an export-oriented nature compared to 30 per cent in the case of FDI projects originating in industrialized countries other than Japan.

A considerable volume of literature in the early 1980s analysed the relative characteristics of FDI from developing countries from a host country's point of view, and brought out a number of positive features. These included a more appropriate scale of operations and technology for the host economy compared to those by foreign enterprises originating in industrialized countries, better utilization of capacity, greater use of local raw materials and skills, and lower consumption of foreign exchange per unit of output. These positive features resulted from the changes made by developing country investing enterprises to the technology imported from abroad to adapt them to the developing country environment and conditions (see, among others, Lall *et al.*, 1983; Wells, 1983; Esho, 1985; Agarwal, 1985. For a review of the findings of these studies, see Kumar, 1986). Wells (1993) found that the differences between developing country-based and industrialized country-based enterprises in Indonesia tended to narrow over time as the former moved increasingly into export-oriented manufacturing.

The emergence of developing country enterprises as outward investors is an important development of the past fifteen years. It widens the options of developing countries looking for FDI inflows and technology, at least in standardized and mature industries. Developing countries are becoming sources not only for domestic market-oriented FDI but also for export-oriented ventures. The least developing countries may find it easier to attract FDI originating in developing countries than FDI from industrialized countries.

CONCLUDING REMARKS AND POLICY IMPLICATIONS

The internationalization theory posits exporting and local production in the host market by either FDI or arm's-length licensing as alternative means of doing business abroad. Host country policies such as protection granted to local industry determine the choice between exporting and local production by MNEs as a mode of serving the local market. The policies also affect the balance between FDI and licensing as a mode for local production. Excessive trade liberalization may prompt MNEs to export rather than produce locally. Liberalization of investment restrictions may change the balance between FDI and licensing in favour of the former as a mode of local production. While a wide range of process technologies, especially those protected by intellectual property rights, is generally easily available on a licensing basis or a contractual basis, technology owners are often wary of providing product technologies, especially those involving the use of brand names unaccompanied by ownership stake and greater control over the management. Hence, the host country policy on foreign brand names may have a bearing on the modes for technology transfer. The contractual or licensing arrangements enable developing host countries to obtain technology unaccompanied by foreign ownership and control over the enterprise and hence allow a greater degree of manoeuvrability. East Asian countries, e.g. South Korea, have been able to build up local technological capability by importing technology on a contractual basis and absorbing and adapting it through reverse engineering (Westphal *et al.*, 1979; Amsden, 1989; Kim, 1997). As will be seen in Chapter 9, this allowed Korean enterprises the independence necessary for pursuing an autonomous path of expansion and internationalization.

An inter-country analysis of FDI inflows reveals that FDI inflows are largely determined by structural factors such as *per capita* income, market size and its growth rate, the extent of industrialization, urbanization, harmonious industrial relations and the quality of infrastructure available, and are adversely affected by economic and political uncertainty. The host country policy factors such as investment incentives and liberalization of policies have a limited role to play in expanding FDI inflows in relatively low-income agrarian economies with low levels of urbanization and poor infrastructure. The recent expansion in the magnitude of FDI inflows in developing countries has benefited a handful of the relatively more industrialized economies in East Asia, Southeast Asia and Latin America, and the low-income countries in South Asia and sub-Saharan Africa continue to receive marginal amounts of FDI despite policy liberalizations. The competition for export-oriented FDI flows is even keener, and the MNEs pick up the winners.

MNE affiliates are found to be having a distinct preference for non-price rivalry including a heavy reliance on marketing, advertising and R&D to differentiate their products, and operate at a larger scale to serve national rather than regional markets. These strategies raise barriers to entry for the new firms and hence adversely affect competition in the local economy. An affiliation with established global chains of companies having a wide range of products and services lends a formidable edge to MNE affiliates over existing local firms. Local firms are pushed to serve price-competitive lower ends of the market, with lower profit margins. Another manner in which MNE entry could affect competition in the host economy is through the spillover effect on competitor local firms. This strand of literature, to be reviewed in Chapter 9, suggests that the nature of the spillover effect depends upon the technological strength of local enterprises. Those local firms that have some technological strength tend to benefit from MNE entry, while the weaker firms are affected adversely and find it harder to survive.

The significant market value of the MNEs' intangible assets, such as established brand names, reputation, etc., may prompt a number of local firms to go in for collaboration with MNEs even if they are technologically self-reliant. In view of the rather strong competitive advantages enjoyed by MNE affiliates, a selective policy towards FDI is appropriate at least in the early stages of a country's industrialization to give protection to local enter-prises while they come up. State intervention to promote healthy competition could also take the form of either offsetting the monopoly power of MNE affiliation and foreign brands through fiscal measures or assisting local firms to build their own brands and technological capability. It is in view of this that some countries attempt to restrict the use of foreign brand names for domestic operations and instead encourage national enter-prises to develop local brand names. In the case of the drugs and pharmaceuticals industry, for instance, some countries encourage the use of generic rather than brand names to curb the market power of MNEs' brand names.

MNEs can also affect market structures in their host countries through other means. In a significant number of cases, foreign entry takes the form of the acquisition of local enterprises, hence affecting the market structures in a more direct manner. Furthermore, market structures in host countries are also affected by international mergers and acquisitions which bring local affiliates of merging MNEs under common control. For instance, recent mergers in the chemical and pharmaceutical industry, such as those between Akzo and Nobel, Glaxo and Wellcome, and Ciba-Geigy and Sandoz, have created bigger companies. These mergers have led to restructuring in the chemical and pharmaceutical industries in all the countries where these

MNEs have affiliates, as the respective affiliates cease to be competitors and are often merged themselves. Hence, market structures in the host countries become more concentrated (see Kumar, 1992a, for examples of increased market concentration in host countries resulting from international mergers and acquisitions). The anti-trust legislations in some industrialized countries do have provisions to control the concentration of market power arising from these mergers. For instance, the US anti-trust legislation reviews all cases of international mergers which may have a potential bearing on US market structures. In cases where the mergers are found to affect US market structures in a significant manner, the MNE may be asked to divest itself of one of the affiliates. The European Commission also has similar anti-trust legislation and power to sanction market dominance. Most developing countries either lack effective anti-trust legislation or their legislation is generally not designed to deal with concentration of market power resulting from overseas mergers. Therefore, the move of developing countries to liberalize their policy framework towards FDI needs to be accompanied by a stronger competition policy which covers anti-trust rules designed to deal with the different ways MNEs can affect market structures, as well as proactive elements such as assisting the local firms in building up their brand names in an attempt to promote healthy competition.

Enterprises from some developing countries have also increasingly used their own outward investments abroad as a means of establishing international linkages. The initial round of developing country FDI flows generally focused on horizontal expansion in other, generally less-developed, countries. Since the mid-1980s these FDI flows have increased rapidly and also show signs of change in their motivation. There is a greater focus on trade supporting FDI in industrialized countries in an effort to gain market access in the face of increasing protectionist barriers. Outward FDI has also been undertaken to improve the price competitiveness of their goods by relocating production in less-developed countries to take advantage of relatively cheap labour or raw materials. In so far as overseas investments of developing country enterprises contribute to increasing the market access of the investing enterprises, their home governments may allow such investments. These investment proposals may be selectively assisted with financing, coverage of non-commercial risks, and avoidance of double taxation of income.

The increasing ability of some developing country enterprises to invest abroad provides an alternative source of FDI flows, including the export-oriented type, for relatively less-developed countries that have been marginalized by FDI flows originating in the industrialized countries. Developing country enterprises are able to provide FDI and technology in a wide range of industries that are maturing. FDI inflows originating in developing countries have been found to have a number of desirable features and may bring in technologies that are more appropriate and adaptable to the market size and factor proportions in developing host countries. Inter-developing country FDI flows also provide an avenue to developing country enterprises on a technological upgrading path to relocate certain labour-intensive industries in which their competitive advantage has been eroded due to rising wages, in other developing countries with cheaper labour availability (see Cooper, 1995, for an empirical analysis of a typology of growth paths adopted by developing countries). Unlike MNEs from the industrialized countries, however, few, if any, enterprises from developing countries enjoy captive information networks. Hence, FDI flows between developing countries may be constrained by the lack of information on investment opportunities in different parts of the world. Therefore, there is scope for institutional intermediation at the international level. On the part of receiving countries, a specific targeting of developing country FDI may be desirable. It is evident that certain countries, e.g. Costa Rica and Colombia, besides the Southeast Asian countries, have recognized the potential of attracting export-oriented FDI from East Asia and have begun to tap this source (Wells, 1993). The efforts at regional economic cooperation among developing countries would also facilitate inter-developing country FDI flows and technology transfers.

8

TECHNOLOGY, MULTINATIONALS AND THE INTERNATIONAL TRADE OF DEVELOPING COUNTRIES

INTRODUCTION

An increasing volume of theoretical and empirical literature has emphasized the role of technology in shaping international trade patterns. The neo-technology theories of international trade, however, have limitations in explaining the trade patterns of developing countries. This chapter examines issues raised in the literature relating to technology and international trade and the recent attempts to extend the theory to explain the trade behaviour of developing country enterprises. In developing countries, technology purchases from abroad are the source of a considerable part of the technologies employed by large firms. Therefore, the role of technology in the trade performance of developing country enterprises has to be examined with respect to both their own technological activities as well as technological purchases from abroad. The latter could be made on an arm's-length basis or as a part of a package of resources within the firm, i.e. as foreign direct investment (FDI). Finally, the chapter also looks into the role of technology in explaining intra-firm trade that accounts for a large and growing proportion of world trade and its implications for developing countries.

The structure of the chapter is as follows. The next section reviews the theoretical and empirical literature on technology and international trade. The chapter goes on to summarize the recent extensions of the theory in defining the role of technology in explaining the trade behaviour of developing country enterprises, and examines the empirical evidence. After that, the possible simultaneity involved in the exports–technology relationship is discussed, with its treatment in the literature. The following section deals with the role of multinational enterprises and FDI in expanding the host country's manufactured exports. It also discusses the role of outward investment as a strategic tool for promoting the international competitiveness of developing country enterprises. The penultimate section summarizes the role of technology in explaining the inter-industry pattern of intra-firm trade and its implications, and the chapter concludes with a few remarks on the policy implications.

TECHNOLOGY AND EXPORTS: THEORY AND EMPIRICAL EVIDENCE

The recent theoretical and empirical literature on international trade has emphasized the contribution of technology and skills to countries' relative competitiveness. In the neo-classical or Heckscher–Ohlin model, the pattern of international trade is determined by the factor endowments; labour-abundant countries specialize in the production and export of labour-intensive goods and import capital-intensive products, and vice versa. Technology was assumed to be given for any industry and accessible to all countries. Although later extensions to the neo-classical model, following Leontief's paradox, incorporated the effect of technological progress on international trade, e.g. the Semuelson–Rybczynski theorem, they made no attempt to understand the causes of technological advance and the possibility of its diffusion across countries. The technology gap theory of Posner (1961) and the subsequent neo-technology theories (Hufbauer, 1966; Vernon, 1966; Krugman, 1979) explicitly consider technological change and its transfer as determinants of a country's international trade pattern (see Dosi *et al.*, 1990; Wangwe, 1992, among others, for recent reviews of the literature).

Posner treated technological change as a continuous process, with time lags between the introduction of a new technology and its adoption elsewhere (imitation lag) and between the development of a new product and the emergence of a demand for it in other countries (demand lag). Therefore, the proposition of Posner is that a continuous process of innovation would give rise to trade even between countries with similar factor endowments and tastes. In a static Heckscher–Ohlin framework there would be no trade between such countries. The argument runs like this: Innovation in a country results in a new product which may be an improvement over an existing product. In due course a demand for that will build up in other countries. Other-country producers may be prevented from producing the new product immediately either by the time required for learning the technology or the know-how involved in making the new product, or by the patent protection enjoyed by the original innovators. So the demand in other countries would be filled by trade in the period of the imitation lag. Therefore, the net effect of imitation lag and demand lag will determine trade, as innovation will not lead to trade in a situation where the demand lag is longer than the imitation lag. Furthermore, innovation causes trade, according to this hypothesis, until other countries catch up with or imitate the new technology. So to sustain its stream of exports, the innovator country will have to keep generating new innovations.

Posner's theory, while linking trade with innovation, could not take into account the possibility of the innovator firms based in a country producing in other countries that may have more appropriate factor endowments by undertaking foreign direct investment. The product-cycle theories proposed by Vernon (1966) and Hirsch (1967) explain the tendency for the production of new goods to be concentrated in the developed economies and its gradual diffusion to other locations. The factor requirements for the production of a good vary over its lifetime, depending upon the stage, and hence one may observe a cycle in its production. Because innovation is a risky business, it is best afforded by industrialized country firms with internal resources and access to relatively high-income consumers who can afford expensive new products. The production of new products in the early stage would also be concentrated in the industrialized economy where the innovation took place and would be exported to other countries. Subsequently, as the product and its manufacturing process become gradually more standardized and as the patent protection, if applicable, expires, producers in other countries will seek to enter the market. In order to retain the markets in other countries, the innovator firm undertakes FDI and makes the product in other industrialized countries. At this stage, exports from the innovating country decline. Finally, when the technology for making the product matures and becomes standardized, and as competition builds up, the need for price competitiveness drives the production to labour-abundant locations which are very often developing countries. The production is moved to developing countries at this stage not only for the local demand in these countries but also to feed the markets in the innovating and other industrialized countries. Hence, exports from developing countries take place at this stage. To put it simply, therefore, the industrialized countries would specialize in the export of new technology-based goods and the developing countries in the export of standardized and matured products.

Krugman (1979) proposed a North–South trade model which posits that innovations occur in the North and new products are produced there, to be produced in the South only after a lag. He argues that new industries must constantly emerge in the North in order to maintain its living standards since the new industries will decline in due course in the face of low-wage competition from the South. The high wages in the North are to some extent the rent on the North's monopoly of new technology. 'This monopoly is continually eroded by technological borrowing and must be maintained by constant innovation of new products . . . the developed region must keep running to stay in the same place' (Krugman, 1979: 262). The evolutionary theorists such as Dosi *et al.* (1990) have further refined the neo-technology theories and have argued that 'technology gaps are of paramount importance in determining the participation of each country in international trade flows and, through that, the maximum levels of income that each country can attain, compatible with the foreign balance constraint' (Dosi *et al.*, 1990: 11). However, they assert that the 'virtuous circle' between technological levels, foreign competitiveness and domestic growth is not entirely automatic and endogenous to the process of development. Country-specific and sector-specific innovative or imitative capabilities can be important factors in giving rise to these virtuous circles, thus explaining the patterns of international convergence or divergence in terms of trade performance and growth performance.

The common feature of almost all the neo-technology models summarized above is the assumption that technology is not a freely, instantaneously and universally available good, and that there are several advantages in being the first. The empirical verification of the technology gap theories has generally been confined to industrialized countries and has typically related cross-sectional trade data with measures of technology intensity. Among the prominent studies, Gruber *et al.* (1967) have found the 'technology factor' to be important in explaining international trade and have observed that the US industries associated with a relatively high 'research effort' also tend to export a relatively high proportion of their output. Caves *et al.* (1980) found net exports of Canadian industries to be significantly related to the industry's R&D intensity.

Soete (1981, 1987), in his studies of forty industries, found the OECD countries' export performance to be a function of their share of patents. Dosi *et al.* (1990: chapter 6) found the percentage change in the number of patents registered in the US by eleven industrial countries to have a significant positive influence on the percentage change in exports (or in balance of trade) in the two periods of time tried, i.e. 1964–80 and 1970–80. In a more recent study probing the role of technology, van Hulst *et al.* (1991) found the patterns of export specialization to be quite similar to those of technological specialization in the case of Germany, Sweden and the Netherlands. Cotsomitis *et al.* (1991), however, using a technology stock variable and time series data, found the technology gap theory unable to predict the direction of high technology trade.

Some studies analysing inter-industry differences in the changes of exports or export intensities have followed an eclectic approach combining both neo-technology and neo-classical theories. Ray (1981), while explaining inter-industry differences in the exports of the USA, introduced industrial organization variables like concentration ratio, scale economies, and product heterogeneity, neo-technology variables like R&D and skill intensities, and government policy variables like tariff and non-tariff barriers, as the main determinants. Ray found the neo-technology and government policy variables important in explaining US exports, but not the industrial organization and neo-classical variables. Sveikauskus (1983) found technology to be a more important factor in explaining US competitiveness than skill and capital intensity.

Hughes (1986), in explaining changes in the export sales ratio of the UK for the period 1972–8, mainly used the neo-technology framework, and introduced the following variables as determinants: R&D intensity, skill intensity, capital intensity, growth in world demand for the products, and changes in export unit values relative to changes in import unit values. All these variables were considered in terms of their average values as well as percentage changes during the period in question. She found the export intensity of UK industries to be significantly related to their R&D and skill intensities and inversely to the average R&D intensity of industry in the USA, France, Germany and Japan. In the same study, the export intensity of German industries was also found to be related to their R&D intensity.

Audrestch and Yamawaki (1988) considered the balance of trade between the USA and Japan as the dependent variable and estimated a regression for a cross-section sample consisting of 213 four-digit manufacturing industries during the late 1970s. The predominant conclusion of their paper was that expenditures by Japanese firms on R&D served as an effective mechanism for promoting the trade balance. Based on their results they contended that R&D expenditure in an industry is not merely a market structure character-istic representing the extent of technological opportunity, but is instead a strategic instrument which can be utilized by the firms to enhance the market share even in a cross-country context. They also found Japanese trade and industrial policy contributing favourably to their trade advantage. They concluded that a part of the Japanese trade success during the 1970s could be ascribed to their import of technology from the USA and the subsequent improvements made by their R&D units. R&D expenditures in the USA and Japan did not have identical impacts on trade balance. Japan was able to derive much more out of its R&D expenditures than was possible by the USA.

Few studies have examined the role of technology in the developing coun-tries' trade. Dasgupta and Siddharthan (1985) found that Indian exports consist largely of standardized goods with a low skill and technological content. In a study explaining the export performance of 100 engineering and forty-five chemical firms, Lall (1986) found R&D expenditure (and not its intensity) to be significant, with a negative sign in the case of engineering firms but with a positive sign in the case of chemical firms. Royalty payments proxying the extent of technology imports and skill intensity had an insignificant coefficient throughout. Kumar (1990a: chapter 6), in his study of forty-three Indian industries, found the technology variable (capturing the intensity of R&D and technology imports) to be not signifi-cant in explaining export performance. Willmore (1992), in a study of 3,764 exporters and 2,826 importers in Brazil, found the existence of R&D not to be significant in explaining either the probability of export or the export performance of exporters. The average wage employed as a proxy of skill intensity turned out with a negative sign but was not significantly different from zero in explaining the probability of export, but was significant with the same sign in explaining the export performance of exporters.

TECHNOLOGY AND TRADE BEHAVIOUR IN DEVELOPING COUNTRIES

The empirical literature reviewed above generally confirms the importance of technology in explaining the trade performance of industrialized countries. In the case of developing countries, however, the neo-technology models have had limited success in explaining export performance. The limitation of the neo-technology models in explaining the trade of developing countries is now widely recognized. This is because early versions of these models were constructed with the purpose of explaining trade among countries at a similar development level (see Goglio, 1993). Krugman (1979), in his version of the technology gap model, brought in the possibility of technology diffusion to explain the North–South trade. New technology is primarily created in the North but is soon diffused to the South. The gap between creation and diffusion creates the possibility of trade. Therefore this model assumes the existence of certain imitative, adaptive or absorptive capability in the South to allow for the diffusion of technological innovations. There is, however, a great variation across the developing countries in terms of local technological capability for imitation, adaptation or absorption. Even within a developing country, industry firms generally differ vastly in terms of the extent of their technological capability. Hence, it may not be possible to deduce a relationship at the industry level.

Kumar and Siddharthan (1994) made an attempt to extend the neo-technology theory to provide an explanation of the role of technology in the export performance of developing country enterprises. They argued that technological activities of developing country enterprises would be important in explaining their export performance only in low- and medium-technology industries. Developing country enterprises are unlikely to achieve a competitive advantage on the basis of their own technological activities in high-technology industries. This is because developing countries are likely to be in an apparently disadvantageous position in the export of high-technology or knowledge-intensive goods. The bulk of R&D activity in most developing countries, with the exception of newly industrializing economies such as South Korea, is adaptive rather than creative in nature. In high-technology industries, the competitive advantage is determined by product innovations which are not the focus of the technological activity of developing country enterprises. The product life-cycles in these industries are usually short, making it difficult to achieve a competitive advantage on the basis of imitation. By the time such product technology diffuses to developing countries it may already be outdated.

The entry of developing country enterprises into the international markets for high-technology goods is also deterred by other barriers such as vertical integration and geographical diversification. The manufacture of high-technology goods contains a significant element of proprietary and firm-specific knowledge (hence these are referred to as S-products by Aharoni and Hirsch, 1993). Marketing of many such products is also associated with a range of highly specialized services such as instruction, installation, repairs, etc., which depend on proprietary knowledge originating with the manufacturer of the goods. The firm-specific nature of the knowledge involved in the product, process and associated services make unbundling difficult. Hence, these industries are dominated by vertically integrated firms that undertake R&D, manufacturing, distribution and servicing in-house or through associated organizations (Aharoni and Hirsch, 1993). The importance of vertical integration thus acts as an entry barrier in these industries.

Furthermore, exporters of high-technology products generally have to be organized to provide product-specific services such as instruction, installation, repairs, maintenance, etc., in the potential markets abroad. This can either be done through an unaffiliated licensee or through an affiliate such as a subsidiary or a branch. If the services are provided through unaffiliated licensees the transaction or governance costs are high because of the risk of losing proprietary knowledge and the need for supervision of quality standards (Kumar, 1990a; Dunning, 1993). The transaction costs can be minimized if the services are provided by the firm's own affiliates. Multinational enterprises, therefore, enjoy an inherent competitive advantage in international markets for high-technology goods because of their in-house ability to provide associated services at geographically diverse locations and savings on transactions costs.

To sum up the above discussion, developing country enterprises are unlikely to achieve a competitive advantage on the basis of their own technological activities in high-technology industries. This is because of their inability to compete through product innovations, shorter product life-cycles, the firm-specific nature of the knowledge and hence significant economies of vertical integration and geographical diversification. The industrialized country enterprises, many of which are multinational in terms of coverage of their operations and are integrated vertically to handle all the tasks related to the production and marketing of high-technology products, reap these economies. The imitative capability that technology gap models assume, therefore, is expected to provide a competitive edge to developing country products only in low- or medium-technology industries. This contention is also consistent with the product cycle theory of Vernon which predicts exports from developing countries to take place in the maturing phases of a product's life when competitive advantage is determined more by factor costs rather than by innovation. That proposition can be generalized to hold good for industries that have reached a relative maturity in terms of technological opportunities, i.e. low- and medium-technology industries.

Kumar and Siddharthan (1994) also verified this contention for a panel data-set for 406 large Indian companies classified in thirteen branches of manufacturing for the period 1987–90. The thirteen industries had been classified according to their relative technology intensity using the UNCTAD classification. The technology factor was captured in terms of in-house R&D and skill intensities. In addition a measure of technology import was employed since Indian firms widely resort to importing to fulfil their technology requirements. Capital intensity of operations was included to examine the role of modernization in export competitiveness. In view of the fact that a large number of Indian enterprises did not export at all, the export performance was explained in the framework of a tobit model. A number of other controls such as firm size and policy variables were also included.

The findings of Kumar and Siddharthan with respect to the main variable capturing technology factor tended to confirm the hypotheses. R&D (or skill) intensity was statistically significant, with a positive sign in medium- or low-technology industries, such as transport equipment, man-made fibres, paper products, rubber products and food processing. These variables were insignificant in all the three high-technology industries. The results tended to support the prediction that, in developing countries such as India, a firm's innovative activity does contribute to export competitiveness in low- and medium-technology industries. In high-technology industries it is beyond the capacity of the developing country enterprises to achieve export competitiveness on the basis of their R&D activity. The insignificance of R&D or skill variables in some medium- and low-technology industries, such as textiles, fabricated metal products, cement and structural clay products, was explained in terms of concentration of R&D activity at equipment manufacturers as in the textiles and cement industries. R&D activity in Indian chemical industries has generally been geared towards process adaptations to accommodate locally available raw materials and feedstocks or the development of indigenous processes for known chemical compounds. These adaptations could be cost-saving in general, but might deter the entry of enterprise in the export markets because of product patents. That explained the indifference of technology variables in explaining the export behaviour of chemical industry firms.

The technology imports variable, on the other hand, was significant with a positive sign in the case of technology-intensive industries, such as non-electrical machinery and electrical machinery industries only. Thus there was some evidence of Indian engineering enterprises breaking into international markets with the help of foreign collaborations or technology imports. In these industries, technology imports usually comprise the import of product designs, which are usually transferred in sub-contracting agreements. The technology import variable was insignificant in all medium- and low-technology industries, except paper and rubber products. In medium- and low-technology industries, technology imports alone appeared unlikely to give Indian enterprises a competitive advantage in export markets.

Another interesting set of findings was with respect to the capital intensity variable. This variable was significant with the hypothesized negative sign in low- and medium-technology industries. On the other hand, in two of the three high-technology industries, electrical engineering and drugs and pharmaceuticals, the capital intensity variable was significant with a positive sign. Kumar and Siddharthan inferred from this finding that, while a higher degree of capital intensity of operations (or automation) did not give a competitive advantage to exporting firms in low- and medium-technology industries, it was desirable for breaking into the export markets in high-technology industries. In other words, enterprises employing labour-intensive processes had an edge over those with more automated production in low- and medium-technology industries, apparently because of low wages prevailing in the country. In high-technology industries, labour-intensive processes appeared to be inefficient despite low wages. This finding is of considerable policy interest and warrants more detailed further work.

TECHNOLOGY AND EXPORTS: DIRECTION OF CAUSATION?

The above analysis emphasizes the role of the technological effort of the enterprises in promoting their export performance. There is also a suggestion in the literature that the relationship could hold good the other way too (Mansfield *et al.*, 1979; Hughes, 1986). A firm serving or wishing to serve the international markets would have a greater need for technological inputs because of the more exacting standards needed to compete there. Hence, they would be more likely to invest in technological effort, especially of the adaptive type. Hughes (1986: 72) has argued that exports will have a positive effect on R&D because the elasticity of export demand with respect to R&D is likely to be greater than the elasticity of domestic demand. Several reasons may lead to export elasticity exceeding that of domestic demand. For instance, because of greater variation between export markets in terms of consumer preferences, entry barriers and elasticities, the likelihood of R&D increasing demand in some of these markets is higher than in the domestic market. Second, if R&D leads to product differentiation or a change in variety that is liked by a small minority of consumers, the economies of scale would imply that this demand would be satisfied by exports. Finally, export demand may be more responsive to R&D than domestic demand, especially if the domestic market is protected.

Among the empirical studies, Mansfield *et al.* reported a significant influence of exports on R&D in a firm-level study of thirty US manufacturing firms. They observed that the firms expected 30 per cent of the R&D returns to come from trade. Hughes (1986) performed a test of simultaneity in the exports–R&D relationship for UK industry for the year 1975, and rejected the hypothesis of no simultaneity. Estimations, whether in a simultaneous equations framework or in simple ordinary least squares, yielded positive significant mutual influence of exports and technology. Among developing country studies, Braga and Willmore (1991) in their Brazilian study and Kumar and Saqib (1996) for their sample of Indian enterprises found export orientation of enterprises to have a significant positive influence in explaining the likelihood of them engaging in R&D activity. These studies, however, did not correct for the possible simultaneity in the relationship.

From the above it seems plausible that the relationship between exports and R&D is of a circular and mutually reinforcing nature. A firm with greater technological effort is more likely to be export-oriented than others; and, once in export markets, it needs more R&D activity. However, the need for more empirical work on resolving the exact nature of the causation is clearly indicated.

MULTINATIONAL ENTERPRISES AND HOST COUNTRIES' EXPORTS

MNEs dominate markets in the industrialized countries and are equipped with captive global information and marketing networks. Therefore, a strong plea is often made that association with MNEs could provide their developing host countries with access to new markets and help in the expansion of manufactured exports. MNEs also rationalize their production across the world in order to take advantage of international differences in factor prices. A number of countries in East and Southeast Asia have been able to expand their manufactured exports by serving as hosts to export platform production for MNEs.

A number of studies have examined the role of MNEs or FDI in the export expansion of developing countries by comparing the relative export performance of foreign-owned and locally-owned enterprises in different countries. The findings of these studies have been mixed. A study of export-oriented firms in South Korea, Taiwan and Singapore by Cohen (1975) concluded that local firms were more likely to export than foreign firms, while that by Riedel (1975) found no significant difference in the export performance of the two groups of firms in Taiwan except in electronics. Some studies compared the proportion of exports in the sales of firms predominantly producing for domestic markets, and found foreign-controlled firms performing more poorly than local firms. The examples include Lall and Streeten (1977) and Subrahmanian and Pillai (1979) for India; Jenkins (1979) for Mexico; and Kirim (1986) for the Turkish pharmaceutical industry. Morgenstern and Mueller (1976) for ten Latin American countries; Newfarmer and Marsh (1981) for the Brazilian electric industry; and Fairchild and Sosin (1986), also for Latin American countries, did not find a significant difference between the export performance of foreign-controlled and local enterprises. Reza *et al.* (1986), in Bangladesh's industrial sector, found foreign firms to be performing better than local firms in terms of exports but also to be highly dependent on imports from parents and other affiliated firms.

Lall and Mohammed (1983b) found a positive, though weak, influence of the degree of foreign ownership on industry's export performance in India. But that did not necessarily imply a superior export performance of MNE affiliates compared to their local counterparts. Lall and Kumar (1981), for a sample of 100 Indian engineering firms, and Lall (1986) for a sample of forty-five Indian chemical industry firms, found foreign share exerting an insignificant effect in the engineering firms sample and a weak positive effect for the chemical firms only in the absence of the technology licences variable with which it was collinear. Kumar (1990a: chapter 4), in his study of forty-three Indian industries, did not find a statistically significant difference in the average or weighted export performance of foreign and local enterprises. A further analysis of the determinants of export performance across the industries did not bring out any significant differences between the industry characteristics of the exports of foreign and local enterprises (Kumar, 1990a: chapter 6; 1987a).

Willmore (1992), using data for a cross-section of 17,053 Brazilian industrial firms, reported that foreign ownership has a large positive effect on both export performance and import propensities, independently of other determinants of trade such as firm size, skill intensity and advertising. Kumar and Siddharthan (1994), in a more recent firm-level analysis of the export performance of Indian enterprises in thirteen Indian industries, found foreign-controlled firms to be performing no better than other firms in all except non-electrical machinery industry. Pant (1995), in a study covering 218 chemical and 202 engineering firms in India, found no significant difference between the export orientation of MNE affiliates and local firms except in the pharmaceutical industry, where local firms actually performed better than foreign firms. Athukorala et al. (1995), in a probit estimation for a sample of 111 manufacturing firms in 1981, found the probability of affiliates of developed country MNEs being exporters significantly no greater than that for local firms, while affiliates of developing country MNEs did reveal a significantly greater probability of being an exporter.

The mixed findings pertaining to the export performance of foreign and local firms across countries may suggest that some countries have been more successful in harnessing the potential of MNEs in expanding manufactured exports. In certain countries, such as Mexico, Taiwan, Hong Kong, Singapore and Malaysia, MNEs have apparently played an important role in expanding manufactured exports from their host countries (Nayyar, 1978; Blomstrom, 1990). Tambunlertchai and Ramstetter (1991) found a significant role played by foreign firms in the export growth of Thailand. In contrast, in India for instance, foreign firms have played a relatively minor role in the expansion of exports with a share of between 5 and 7 per cent of India's exports (Rao, 1994). What are the factors that explain the divergent performance of MNEs across countries in terms of export orientation? The success of some countries in expanding manufactured exports is in fact due to their ability to attract export-oriented FDI. The latter represents investments made by MNEs to relocate their production away from home countries or other industrialized countries in response to rising wage costs. In Malaysia and Indonesia, for instance, about 70 per cent of the projects involving FDI have been export-oriented. In China, the share of foreign-owned firms soared from a negligible 0.3 per cent in 1984, to 5 per cent in 1988, to 30 per cent by 1993 (Chen *et al.*, 1995). Thus only export-oriented FDI and not FDI as such may help in export promotion in host countries.

Export-oriented FDI arises in the process of relocation of production by MNEs abroad in order to maintain their international competitiveness in the face of rising wages and other costs, currency appreciations and the increasing costs of pollution abatement in their home countries. The relocation of production is attempted sometimes through sub-contracting to unaffiliated enterprises and sometimes through affiliates set up abroad to undertake production meant for exports. Arm's-length international sub-contracting and export-oriented FDI are, therefore, two principal alternative means of expanding manufactured exports for developing countries. Sub-contracting of production abroad entails the transfer of knowledge, designs, drawings, specifications and quality control. Because of this the relative importance of arm's-length sub-contracting and export-oriented FDI varies a great deal across industrial sectors, depending upon the governance or transaction costs involved. In cases where the transaction costs are high, for instance, because of a closely held novel technology or knowledge, the subcontractor may prefer overseas production by means of a subsidiary (i.e., FDI) rather than arm's-length sub-contracting to avoid the risk of losing a trade secret, e.g. in microchip fabrication. In more standardized products such as leather goods or textiles, contracts are generally fairly easy to govern. Hence, sub-contracting to unaffiliated parties is fairly common for these products. In an econometric analysis, Siddharthan and Kumar (1990) found intra-firm trade between US MNEs and their affiliates abroad to be predominating the R&D and skill-intensive industries. In these knowledge- or technology-intensive industries, therefore, export-oriented FDI would be a principal channel of tapping the market access of MNEs by developing countries.

There is an intense competition among countries to attract export-oriented or export platform production from MNEs by offering various incentives and attractions. A large number of export processing zones have been set up in different parts of the world to attract export platform investments from MNEs. Kumar (1994a), in an empirical analysis of the inter-country pattern of the export-oriented investments made by US MNEs across forty countries, found the extent of export-oriented investment attracted by a country to be determined by wage levels, industrial capability, infrastructure and the presence of export processing zones. The government policy towards FDI (e.g. incentives and performance obligations) or the overall international orientation of the economy did not affect it significantly.

In an analysis of export-oriented FDI made by US and Japanese enterprises abroad, Kumar (1996a) observed a recent stagnation in these flows because of the evolution of new manufacturing and organizational techniques. This, however, does not diminish the prospects for attracting these investments for developing countries which have been unsuccessful in attracting them so far. This is because of the foot-loose nature of these investments, as revealed by their changing geographical pattern. Southeast Asian countries such as Malaysia, Indonesia, Thailand and China have successfully replaced the East Asian newly industrializing economies, Hong Kong, Korea, Taiwan and Singapore, as the most important hosts of export-oriented FDI in Asia. South Asian countries have failed to attract any significant volume of export-oriented FDIs despite an abundance of cheap labour and skills. The study also finds that preferential access to home country market and partnerships in regional economic and trading cooperation schemes is becoming an increasingly important attraction for these FDIs.

Outward investment and exports

Besides affiliating with MNEs through inward FDI or sub-contracting or licensing arrangements, another way of securing 'proprietary associations abroad', that is of critical significance for exports of especially skill-intensive products (Hirsch, 1970), is by setting up affiliates abroad that support the export effort of enterprises. As seen in the previous chapter, one of the major motivations for developing country enterprises to invest abroad is trade supporting. The overseas affiliates also help the enterprises receive an 'insider' status in the regional trading blocs that are being formed by the industrialized countries in Europe and North America, and hence defend their markets in the face of rising protectionist barriers (see Kumar, 1994c, for illustrations). This probably explains the rising concentration of outward FDI of developing countries in industrialized countries which are their principal markets, as was reported in Table 7.2. The recent acceleration of outward FDI flows from developing countries, as reported in UNCTAD (1995), is partly due to the increasing trade supporting investments undertaken abroad by developing country enterprises. Enterprises in the East Asian newly industrializing economies are also using outward FDI to improve the price competitiveness of their goods, which has suffered adversely from rising wages and currency appreciations, by moving their production to cheap-labour locations. Sometimes these investments are also driven by the availability of preferential access to major markets, e.g. in the Mediterranean, East or Central European, or Lome Convention countries, that enjoy preferential access to the European Union market, or in countries that have unfulfilled MFA quotas in the garments and textiles industry (Kumar, 1995c). Agarwal (1985) provided some evidence on the operations of Indian enterprises abroad having a positive effect on India's exports. Rigorous empirical evidence on the role and efficacy of outward FDI in securing the international competitiveness of developing country enterprises is still lacking. However, with increasing protectionism and growing emphasis on the internationalization of operations, it seems certain that more enterprises from developing countries would employ outward investments as a strategic tool for strengthening their presence abroad in the coming years.

TECHNOLOGY AND INTRA-FIRM TRADE

The growing relocation of production by MNEs explains the rising importance of intra-firm trade in world trade. Intra-firm trade, defined as trade between the parent MNE and its affiliates, accounts for anything between a third and a half of total world trade, and an even larger proportion of trade in many high-technology goods. Intra-firm trade has been explained in terms of the breakdown of markets in the trade of some goods characterized by high transaction, and hence the supplanting of market by the internal structure of the firm. Transaction costs are generally high in the export of knowledge-intensive products due to product novelty, problems in codification of knowledge and buyer uncertainty, among other factors.

A few studies have analysed the determinants of inter-industry variations in the significance of intra-firm exports and imports in terms of industry characteristics. Lall (1978b) analysed the determinants of the inter-industry pattern of intra-firm exports by US MNEs during 1970. His results showed R&D intensity to be the most prominent variable in explaining US exports. The other important variables were the extent of internationalization of the US industry, and tariff policy. Thus, even during the 1970s, technology-intensive goods were exported by US corporations to their affiliates intra-firm and not through the normal open market channels. Only standardized products were traded through the open international market.

Helleiner and Lavergne (1979) analysed the determinants of intra-firm imports of US corporations for the years 1975 and 1977. As in the case of exports, imports also were dominated by R&D-intensive industries. Their results revealed that related party imports were a significantly higher proportion of US imports in industries where the skill intensity and R&D intensity were high. They also separately estimated equations for intra-firm imports from OECD countries and intra-firm imports from developing countries. The results from the OECD countries were similar to that of the overall imports. But, in the case of the intra-firm imports from developing countries, the only significant determinant was R&D intensity. Helleiner and

Lavergne also tried to explain the percentage change in intra-firm imports between 1975 and 1977. Even here the most important determinant was R&D. They concluded that 'the apparently increasing role of industries involved in R&D in intra-firm importing from developing countries is . . . striking' (Helleiner and Lavergne, 1979: 305).

With Lall focusing on intra-firm exports, and Helleiner and Lavergne on intra-firm imports, a unified treatment of both these dimensions of trade in a comprehensive framework was lacking. Siddharthan and Kumar (1990) analysed the proportion of intra-firm trade (both exports and imports) in the total trade of the US MNEs (parents) across thirty-two branches of manufacturing with the help of the US Department of Commerce's 1982 Benchmark Survey Data on US Direct Investments Abroad. The study employed the transaction cost minimization paradigm to formulate the hypotheses. The internalization advantages seemed particularly high in R&D and skill-intensive industries. In the empirical analysis, R&D intensity emerged as the most prominent determinant for both intra-firm exports and intra-firm imports. The results of the determinants of intra-firm trade diverged from those of international trade (exports and imports) in several respects. Other industry characteristics like capital requirements that were influential in explaining the international trade pattern among nations were not important in determining intra-firm trade. The primary reason for this difference is that intra-firm trade is predominantly due to market failures and internalization advantages, while trade through the market is due to the differences in the comparative costs and resource endowments. If there are no internalization advantages in the variables influencing comparative costs and representing resource endowments, then in all such cases trade through the market would be preferred. The results also revealed that the proportion of intra-firm exports from the USA was sizeable in industries that necessitated large selling and market development expenditures. Bonturi and Fukasaku (1993), in an OECD study, re-estimated Siddharthan and Kumar's model with the 1989 Benchmark survey data of intra-firm trade of US corporations, and, except for the pollution intensity variable, all their findings echoed the original results for the 1982 data. The different measurement of pollution intensity employed by the two studies perhaps made this variable behave differently. Sleuwaegen and Yamawaki (1991) contrasted the data on Japanese intra-firm trade with that of US corporations, and found that Japanese parent firms imported relatively less from their foreign affiliates and directed their intra-firm exports strongly to their foreign distribution subsidiaries in the USA and Europe. This type of intra-firm trade is self liquidating in nature, as it is substituted over time by local manufacturing when the market grows, and transportation costs and trade restrictions increase.

One implication of the finding of concentration of intra-firm trade in knowledge- and marketing-intensive industries is that relocation of production by MNEs in these industries would be undertaken largely through FDI. Arm's-length sub-contracting may be resorted to in other industries. Therefore, countries seeking to expand manufactured exports with the help of MNEs will have to attract export platform FDI in knowledge-intensive industries. Sub-contracting arrangements entered into between local firms and overseas corporations may help in expanding exports of other manufactured goods.

CONCLUDING REMARKS AND POLICY IMPLICATIONS

Recent theoretical and empirical literature has placed a lot of emphasis on the role of the technological activities of firms in shaping their, and hence their home country's, international competitiveness. Even though the neo-technology theories were formulated for explaining industrialized countries' trade, the technological effort of developing country enterprises has been found to be important in explaining their export performance in medium- and low-technology industries. It is this fact that explains the blurring of boundaries between the technology and trade policies that Mowery and Rosenberg (1989: 274) have noted. The two-way causation between exports and R&D, as has been noted by several studies, may also explain the blurring of the distinction between these policies. Governments in the most industrialized and industrializing countries pursue 'policies to promote innovation and technological advance' of their enterprises in an effort to strengthen their country's international competitiveness. In the recent years, the activist or aggressive trade policies adopted by the governments of many industrialized countries to sharpen the competitive edge of national enterprises has been rationalized under the so-called 'new trade theory' or 'strategic trade theory' (see Panchamukhi, 1994). It has been shown that, under conditions of imperfect competition, a nation can significantly alter its comparative advantage and its world trading position by suitable strategic interventions that affect R&D, technology and the market power of enterprises (see Helpman and Krugman, 1989). The menu of strategies to enhance the export competitiveness of their industries employed by governments in recent times is quite large, and includes subsidization of R&D and worker education, to enhance the technological capabilities and productivity of domestic industries, and the search for stronger protection of intellectual property (see Scherer and Belous, 1994: 35–8, for examples and details). Other strategic policies that have been employed include commodity export subsidies, subsidized export financing, the provision of cheap raw materials, learning curve pricing strategies, cartel formation and dumping, the protection of home markets to allow scale economies to domestic industries, coordination of industry investments to ensure scale economies, coercive market opening measures, and trade-supporting macroeconomic policies (see Scherer and Belous, 1994: chapter 5). Developing country governments could similarly promote the technological effort of their enterprises, which may improve their international competitiveness.

Strategic affiliations with multinational enterprises is another way of promoting the international competitiveness of enterprises in developing countries. The role of MNEs in expanding the manufactured exports of their host countries, however, varies widely across countries. Some countries have been more successful than others in expanding their exports with the help of MNEs. The diverging performance of countries in this respect is explained in terms of the differences in the ability of the countries to attract export-oriented or export platform FDI. Export-oriented FDI alone helps host countries in expanding their exports. Export-oriented FDI is a special type of FDI determined by factors different from those influencing domestic market-oriented FDI flows. Hence, countries seeking market access from MNEs target export-oriented FDI inflows or enter into sub-contracting arrangements with MNEs. Research on intra-firm trade, which is related to the relocation of production and overseas processing for exports or export-oriented FDI, has shown that technology-intensive products are more likely to be traded on an intra-firm basis. In other words, it may be more difficult to sub-contract production from MNEs for exports of technology-intensive products than for relatively standardized and matured products. These considerations may be taken into account by a policy on the expansion of manufactured exports. Developing country enterprises, especially the East Asian ones, are also strengthening their international competitiveness by making investments in trade-supporting affiliates abroad. Outward FDI as a strategic tool may become more important for developing country enterprises for expanding their markets abroad in future with the growing emphasis on internationalization and increasing protectionism.

9

TECHNOLOGY IMPORTS AND DOMESTIC TECHNOLOGICAL CAPABILITY IN HOST COUNTRIES

INTRODUCTION

The issue of the impact of technology imports on local technological capability, whether in the form of technology licensing contracts or as a part of a package of FDI, is a complex one. There are a number of ways in which imported technology could contribute to building local capability in the host country. Technology transfer benefits most immediately the importing firms. However, the knowledge that is transferred under most technology transfer agreements is generally restricted to production know-how. The capability to adapt, constantly to update the product and process, and to innovate further, is hardly ever transferred under contracts but is acquired in the process of absorption and assimilation of the imported technology in in-house R&D activity. Therefore, the nature of the interface between technology imports and local R&D is of crucial importance from the point of view of building local technological capabilities in importing countries. The imported technologies may have significant externalities for the host economy and may also be diffused among and benefit firms other than those importing it. Evidence suggests that considerable knowledge and productivity spillovers do take place from technology imports in the host economy. Finally, another mechanism of the diffusion of technology in the host economy is through vertical inter-firm linkages and mobility of employees. This chapter examines these issues in some detail and reviews the evidence provided by recent studies.

The next section discusses the issues involved in determining the nature of the relationship between technology imports and local R&D, and summarizes the empirical evidence reported by the numerous studies on the subject. After that, the chapter examines the issues concerning knowledge spillovers from FDI and technology transfer contracts, and the evidence thereon. The following section discusses the diffusion of knowledge from FDI in the host country through vertical inter-firm linkages and training and mobility of employees, while the final section summarizes the policy implications.

TECHNOLOGY IMPORTS AND IN-HOUSE R&D: COMPLEMENTS OR SUBSTITUTES?

The nature of the relationship between technology imports and local in-house R&D has been a subject of increasing debate in recent development literature. One school of thought has tended to view technology imports as a substitute for local R&D activities. Therefore, excessive technology imports could be inimical to the building-up of local technological capabilities. On the other hand, an importer of technology generally needs to supplement it by in-house technological effort to absorb and adapt the purchased knowledge. Therefore, technology imports and local technological efforts are considered as complementary to each other, according to the other view (see also Evenson and Westphal, 1995, for a recent survey).

Blumenthal (1979) argued that the technological level of a country is a function of indigenous R&D, technology imports, and the relation between the two. She found the relationship to be a complex one, depending, among other things, upon the nature of R&D, the degree of risk aversion of private firms, the role played by the government in high-risk projects, the relative expenditure on basic as opposed to applied research, the availability of foreign technology and the government policy towards it, the institutional framework for adaptation of technology, and the industry structure. Consequently, Blumenthal's empirical exercise for six countries, Australia, France, West Germany, Italy, Japan, and Sweden, led to no firm conclusion. For three countries, i.e. Australia, Japan and France, there is evidence of complementarity between imported technology and local R&D, while no significant relationship was found in the case of the other three countries.

Odagiri (1983) analysed the relationship between R&D expenditures and patent royalty payments. In particular he sought an answer to the main question, 'Are R&D expenditures and royalty payments substitutes or complements?' (Odagiri, 1983: 61). He argued in favour of considering royalty payments as a substitute for R&D, and hypothesized a negative relationship between the two variables. In his view, firms made a choice between conducting research themselves and procuring technology from outside against royalty and other payments. Hence they should be considered alternative means of paying for research. His sample consisted of 370 Japanese manufacturing firms. Contrary to his hypothesis, his statistical results showed a positive relationship between R&D expenditures and expenditures on royalty payments, both expressed as a percentage of sales. Subsequent scrutiny of the data revealed that the drug industry, in relation to the volume of sales, not only spent more on R&D but also made larger payments to other firms for obtaining licences for patents, mostly to foreign companies. Other industries where both these expenditures were high included precision equipment, chemical and electrical equipment. He categorized these four industries as innovators, and the other nine industries in his study as non-innovators. In his definition, innovators were those who carried out innovative R&D, while non-innovators undertook adaptive R&D. On an average, the innovators spent 1–2 per cent of sales on R&D and the non-innovators spent 0.2–0.4 per cent on R&D. Both groups spent much less on royalty. When separate equations were estimated for these two groups, a positive relationship emerged for R&D and royalty payments, but the relationship was significant only for the non-innovators. Hence, Odagiri concluded that, for the non-innovators performing adaptive R&D, import of technology was complementary to in-house research, but was not so for firms performing innovative research.

Lall (1983) examined the determinants of R&D in the Indian engineering industry, hypothesizing a positive relationship between technology imports and in-house R&D, which is largely of an adaptive nature in countries like India. He used two separate variables to represent technology imports, namely, the number of foreign licensing agreements entered into by a firm, and the royalties paid deflated by sales. In his equations explaining R&D intensity, the coefficient of both the variables had positive signs indicating a complementary relationship, although only the coefficient of royalty payments was statistically significant. Foreign ownership also had a positive sign but was significant at the 10 per cent level only.

A number of studies have investigated the relationship between technology imports and in-house R&D across industries. Katrak (1985), in line with earlier studies (Desai, 1980; Lall, 1983) maintained that Indian R&D is basically adaptive and consequently the import of technology would encourage in-house R&D. His regression results based on forty-three industry-level observations for India showed a complementary relationship between the import of technology and R&D expenditures in tune with the 'import and adapt' technology strategy. The results were similar for both the variables employed to denote technology imports, i.e. the import of equipment and royalty and technical fee payments. His main conclusion was that technology imports stimulated in-house R&D, but its effect was rather limited, especially for complex technologies. The latter finding was explained in terms of the limited technological capability of Indian firms in the adaptation of relatively complex technologies.

Kumar (1987b) argued that the nature of the relationship between imported technology and local R&D is also influenced by the mode of technology import, in addition to other factors. Firms importing technology internally, i.e. under a package of foreign direct investment (FDI), may not be induced to invest in R&D because of their continued captive access to the centralized research laboratories of the MNEs. On the other hand, unaffiliated licensees may be prompted to invest in R&D not only by the lack of access to the parent's laboratories but also by the anxiety to absorb technology during the life of the licensing agreement. Therefore, technology imported through FDI may not be followed by local R&D, while licensing imports may be complemented by further technological effort. Hence, the FDI mode may be characterized by substitution and licensing by complementarity. MNEs also tend to centralize their R&D activity near their headquarters and may discourage their affiliates in developing countries from undertaking in-house R&D activity. This proposition was put to test in an inter-industry study. Kumar estimated an R&D function for a cross-section of forty-three Indian industries (at a three digit level of disaggregation) for the years 1978–81. Two technology import variables were included in this study: the share of foreign-controlled enterprises in industry sales representing the importance of FDI, and the proportion of royalty and technical fees remitted abroad. Both these variables were significant in explaining the variation in R&D intensity – foreign share with a negative – and royalty payments with a positive sign, thus upholding the contention that technology import through FDI may not be followed by in-house R&D and could have a depressing effect on the levels of local R&D spending, while unaffiliated licensees may be more willing to absorb, assimilate and master imported technologies.

Desai (1980: 85; 1985: 2086) has also observed that many Indian firms stepped up their R&D outlays after their technology import agreements expired and government approval for their extension was difficult to get; some others did so after their technology suppliers failed to help them. In view of the trends in Indian industry under changing policies in the 1980s, Subrahmanian (1991) noted that firms develop their technological capability under protectionism and regulation differently than under economic liberalism. In the former, firms supplement their technology imports by internal R&D effort and strengthen their manufacturing capability, although the building-up of design capability needed for continuous updating is neglected because of protection. Under a liberal economic environment firms will build up technological capability through continued reliance on technology imports. In other words, the technology imports may not be complemented by internal R&D in a liberal policy environment.

Deolalikar and Evenson (1989) made use of an industry-level data-set for fifty Indian industries over the period 1960–70, and estimated an input demand system based on a generalized quadratic cost function where R&D (measured in terms of patents taken out by Indian industry) and technology purchase are treated as jointly determined by characteristics of Indian industries, prices, and supply of purchasable foreign technology. They found some evidence of the complementarity of purchased technology and inventive activity. Foreign and state ownership did not have a significant relationship with domestic patenting in the country, except for the chemical industry. In the chemical industry, domestic patenting was positively related with state ownership and negatively so with foreign ownership. Deolalikar and Evenson explained the latter as the tendency of MNEs in the drug industry to use their parent company's inventions in India and avoid carrying out R&D in India. The state ownership's sign was positive in view of the avowed objective of the public sector entry in the drugs sector to reduce the dependence of the country on foreign technology and MNEs.

Siddharthan (1988) examined the R&D activity of firms in the Indian chemical, electronic, industrial machinery and textile industries. Within each industry, he separated firms on the basis of ownership – private or public. The proportion in sales of lump-sum payments for technology as provided in foreign collaboration approvals for the years 1982–5 denoted technology imports and the proportion of R&D expenditure was the dependent variable. The relationship between the import of technology and in-house R&D varied across industries as well as across ownership groups, thus casting a doubt on the robustness of the cross-section industry results. The coefficient of the import of technology variable had a positive sign for the private sector firms for all the industries, though it was not significantly different from zero for heavy machinery and chemical industry firms. However, in the case of the full sample, the technology import coefficient was not significant. For the private sector firms the evidence showed a mild complementary relationship between in-house R&D and technology imports. The public sector firms seemed to have a negative relationship between the import of technology and in-house R&D efforts

Katrak (1990) considered a sample of fifty-six technology-importing Indian firms operating in the electrical, electronic and machinery industries (based on data collected by NCAER), and analysed their R&D behaviour. Technology imports were represented by the number and not the value of foreign collaborations. In addition, a dummy variable that took the value 1 if the type of technology imported included those intended to strengthen in-house R&D, and another one which took the value 1 if the importer had exclusive rights, were included. In the regression equations the first two variables had positive signs while the last one had a negative sign. Nevertheless, based on these results, Katrak concluded that R&D expenditures were higher in enterprises where technology imports were intended to strengthen the R&D units. Based on the negative coefficient for the last variable he concluded that technological effort was lower in enterprises that negotiated an exclusive right of sale in the home market. However, these results should be taken as conjectures in view of the limitations of measurements as well as low levels of statistical significance.

Braga and Willmore (1991), in a study covering 4,342 establishments in Brazil, analysed the probability of a firm doing in-house R&D in the framework of a logit model. The empirical results reveal that firms importing technology were more likely to undertake R&D than others. Firm size, diversification and export-orientation also favoured R&D significantly, while foreign or state ownership, profitability, protection and market concentration did not have any significant influence. However, foreign-owned firms and technology importers showed a greater tendency to have a systematic programme of new product development.

Siddharthan (1992) used firm-level data for a sample of sixty-nine Indian private sector firms reporting R&D expenditure for the period 1985–7, and used foreign equity participation and lump-sum payments as a percentage of sales turnover as technology import variables to explain R&D intensity. The coefficients of both the variables were positive and significant, implying a complementary relationship between technology imports and R&D. The value of the coefficient of foreign equity participation, however, was less than that of the coefficient of lump-sum payments. It is, however, not possible to infer anything about the differential impact of technology imports through internal and market means, as the samples of firms had not been separated.

Kumar and Saqib (1996) examined the relationship between technology imports and local R&D activity for a sample of 291 firms included in the RBI survey of foreign collaborations in the framework of probit and tobit models. They measured technology imports through the proportion of royalties and technology fees in net sales, in common with most studies. In addition, a dummy variable separating foreign-controlled firms was employed to examine whether these enterprises behaved differently from those importing technology through arm's-length channels. In the empirical exercise, however, neither of the two variables achieved statistical significance, implying that the relationship between technology imports and local R&D varied across firms and neither complementarity nor substitution dominated the relationship.

Arora (1991) questioned the tendency in the literature to infer from a positive correlation between technology imports and R&D expenditures in cross-section studies that the two decisions were complementary. He developed a framework which implied that further restrictions were necessary in order that this interpretation be valid, and suggested some plausible conditions under which complementarity would imply a positive correlation in such regressions. Fikkert (1993) also argued that most studies of technology import and in-house R&D interaction suffered from sampling biases, and from a problem of simultaneity in that they treated one of the two as an exogenous variable. He treated R&D and foreign technology purchase as jointly determined by including cross-equation and exclusionary restrictions in the model in his study covering 305 Indian private sector firms for the period 1974–8. His empirical results showed that: technology imports and R&D have a significant negative relationship; firms having foreign equity participation have an insignificant direct effect on R&D but they tend to depend significantly more on foreign technology purchases, which in turn tend to reduce R&D; and trade restrictions have induced adaptive R&D. In view of these findings, he concluded that 'India's closed technology policies with respect to foreign direct investment and technology licensing had the desired effect of promoting indigenous R&D, the usual measure of technological self-reliance'. Furthermore, in view of the evidence of Indian R&D

absorbing considerable foreign R&D spillover, he suggested that a 'weak patent regime may allow spillovers simultaneously to promote R&D and to have a positive direct effect on productivity', and implied that the adoption of a 'stronger patent regime may not be optimal from either the short- or long-run perspectives'. To some extent, Fikkert's results corroborate those of Kumar (1987b), where he found an adverse effect of FDI on R&D. In the light of his results, and in common with Kumar (1990c), he also felt that a tax on technology imports could improve welfare.

These results, therefore, tend to highlight Blumenthal's assertion that the complexity of the relationship depends upon many factors. There are some technology imports that are followed by local R&D and there are others which eliminate the need to carry out R&D. The complexity of the relationship suggests that much is to be learnt from case studies. A factor that turns out to be important in determining the nature of the relationship is the mode of technology imports. In the internal, or FDI, mode of technology imports, the technology supplier retains the controlling stake in the enterprise. The bulk of FDI flows world-wide is associated with MNEs. The technology-recipient enterprise becomes a link in the global chain of affiliates subject to centralized decision-making. The location of R&D, as that of production and sourcing, is generally subject to centralized decision-making, owing to its strategic importance to global operations. Hence, the affiliate in a developing country undertakes local R&D only if it fits into the global strategy of the enterprise. Though over the years MNEs have shown a tendency to decentralize their R&D activity geographically, it is still concentrated largely in the industrialized countries. A marginal proportion of the R&D of MNEs that takes place in developing countries is concentrated in those countries that are able to offer them cheaper technological resources and infrastructure (Kumar, 1996b).

KNOWLEDGE SPILLOVERS FROM FDI AND TECHNOLOGY TRANSFERS

An important indirect consequence of FDI and technology licensing contracts on host economies could be in the form of spillovers of knowledge to locally-owned firms. These may include exposure to new production or management technologies employed by foreign firms and spillovers of knowledge through employee mobility. In certain cases the demonstration effect from foreign firms may be speeding up the diffusion of new technologies. Yet another source of spillovers could be through the increased competition from foreign entry which forces local firms to become more efficient users of existing technologies or to explore new technologies. These spillovers could constitute an important positive externality of FDI on the host economies.

There have been two strands of empirical literature that have attempted to capture these different sources of spillovers from MNEs in their host countries. The first group includes studies that attempted quantitatively to analyse the impact of foreign entry or presence on the productivity or efficiency of local firms. Some of these studies used multiple regression analysis to detect the effect of technology imports on the productivity of non-importing firms. The other set attempted to analyse the knowledge spillovers from R&D and technology imports with the help of production functions. The second group of studies includes those examining the backward and forward linkage generation by MNE affiliates and the training and employee mobility which are also sources of knowledge spillovers. These studies have generally adopted a case study approach.

Knowledge spillovers and productivity improvements

Caves (1974b) attempted to evaluate the presence of these spillovers in Australian manufacturing industry by examining the effect of foreign share in an industry on the labour productivity of locally-owned firms. The effect was found to be positive. Globerman (1979) found weaker evidence of the presence of technical efficiency spillovers in Canadian industry using Caves's methodology. Blomström (1989: chapter 4) found a strong positive association between the labour productivity of owned enterprises and foreign share in employment in 1970 in 215 four-digit Mexican manufacturing industries. However, foreign entry (defined in terms of change in foreign share between 1970 and 1975) was not found to be related to changes in the technological frontier nor changes in the labour productivity of the least efficient plants. Blomström and Wolff (1989), in a further work on twenty two-digit Mexican industries for the period 1965–84, found increasing convergence of the productivity levels of locally-owned firms to that of foreign-owned firms. The rate of growth of productivity of local firms was found to be positively related to the degree of foreign ownership of an industry. Furthermore, they found evidence of convergence of the productivity levels between Mexican and US industries over the period and the rate of convergence was related to the extent of foreign ownership in the industries. One should keep in mind, however, an important limitation of inter-sectoral studies, i.e. the potential overestimation of the positive impact of foreign presence on the domestic firms' productivity if the FDI was concentrated in more productive industries.

Haddad and Harrison (1993) examined the impact of FDI on the productivity of firms in Morocco's manufacturing sector using a firm-level panel data-set for 1985–9 which allowed controlling for firm-specific influences such as firm size. They found that, after controlling for firm size, foreign firms do not exhibit higher levels of labour productivity or a greater outward orientation for most sectors, although they do continue to pay higher real wages than domestically-owned firms. Foreign firms achieved on average a higher level of total factor productivity than local firms, but the growth rate of their productivity was not higher. Haddad and Harrison found evidence that sectors with high levels of FDI have a lower dispersion of productivity levels across firms, moving domestic firms closer to the efficiency frontier. However, no significant relationship was found between higher productivity growth in domestic firms and greater foreign presence in a sector. The faster productivity growth of domestic firms could not be attributed to a higher foreign share.

Aitken and Harrison (1993) reproduced a similar exercise for panel data on 4,000 Venezuelan firms for the period 1975–89. In Venezuela, foreign-owned firms exhibited on average higher labour productivity, higher propensity to import as well as export and paid higher wages than their domestic counterparts, even after controlling for size and capital intensity, etc. Foreign ownership was found to affect the productivity of domestically-owned plants in Venezuela. The negative effects were large and robust. These results suggest that the benefits of FDI are limited to direct effects on productivity improvements with improved technology by enterprises receiving foreign participation, and spillovers to other local enterprises are negligible and do not justify the incentives granted by host governments to foreign investors.

Kokko (1994), examining Mexican data, found no evidence of spillovers in industries where foreign affiliates had a much higher productivity and larger market shares than local firms. In other industries, there appeared to be a positive relationship between foreign presence and local productivity. This result suggests that spillovers from foreign enterprises are dependent upon local capability in the industry. If local firms are too weak they will not be able to absorb spillovers and might vanish in the face of competition from foreign firms, as Cantwell (1989) observed in a study of the impact of the entry of US firms in European markets between 1955 and 1975. He found that the entry of US affiliates provided a highly beneficial competitive spur in the industries where local firms had some traditional technological strength, whereas local firms in other industries were forced out of business or pushed to the market segments neglected by MNEs.

Mixed evidence from different countries on knowledge spillovers from FDI again suggests that the impact of FDI varies a great deal across countries. Some countries seem to have been better able to harness the positive externalities of FDI than others.

Productivity improvements and rates of returns of technology acquisition

Some studies have used the production function approach to estimate the marginal products of R&D, technology imports and their spillovers to other firms following the tradition of studies made for the US and Canada (see Griliches, 1995, for a recent survey). Basant and Fikkert (1996), in a study covering panel data for 787 large Indian private-sector firms for the period 1974–82, estimated the impact of in-house R&D, expenditures on foreign technology purchase and spillovers of foreign and domestic R&D on productivity. They controlled for firm-level heterogeneity through fixed effects estimation. They found quite high rates of return to both R&D and technology purchase expenditures. While the private returns to technology imports ranged between 124 and 165 per cent, depending upon the specification, the returns to own R&D varied between 19 and 80 per cent and were highly sensitive to the specification. The R&D activity of other domestic firms tended to have a significant positive impact on output, while foreign R&D activity significantly raised the marginal productivity of in-house R&D. In view of the fact that local R&D, especially of the type that is conducted at rather modest levels and is geared to specific product and process adaptations by developing country enterprises, is known to have rather high returns, a rather small and highly unstable estimate compared to that for technology imports is somewhat surprising. Since the sales data are used to estimate output, a part of the return may represent the quasi-rents associated with foreign brand names that often accompany foreign technologies.

In a more recent study, Haksar (1995) estimated marginal products of R&D and technology imports – both embodied in capital goods imports and disembodied – and their spillover effects on other firms' productivities, using Reserve Bank of India data for 642 Indian firms distributed across sixty-five industries for the period 1975–90. His estimates indicate a 141 per cent rate of return on own R&D, nearly 30 per cent return on disembodied technology import expenditures, and 9 per cent on embodied technology imports. Both local R&D and disembodied technology imports had positive spillovers which made their social rates of return higher than their private returns, i.e. 145 and 45 per cent respectively. Therefore, although (disembodied) technology imports had a much smaller rate of return to the importer than similar investments in R&D, the spillovers to other firms were quite substantial. Haksar also estimated these rates for specific sectors and found them to be even larger for the scientific industries, but broadly bearing the same pattern. For the pharmaceutical industry the private and social rates of return to R&D were by far the highest, at 173 and 198 per cent respectively. He explained this in terms of the highly successful adaptive R&D effort of Indian pharmaceutical industry firms directed at the development of alternative processes of known drugs. This has been made possible by weak patent laws which did not allow patents on pharmaceutical products. Incidentally, technology imports had rather poor rates of return at 22 per cent and there were hardly any spillovers in this industry. Ferrantino (1992) examined the effect of expenditure and technology purchase on costs in Indian manufacturing using firm-level data for the 1975–81 period. His results revealed no systematic relationship between technology imports and efficiency of firms.

VERTICAL INTER-FIRM LINKAGES WITH THE DOMESTIC ECONOMY

The vertical inter-firm linkages created by foreign enterprises could be an important externality for the host economy and could also be sources of the diffusion of knowledge from them. Katz (1969), for instance, noted that the inflow of FDI into the Argentine manufacturing sector in the 1950s had a significant impact on the technologies used by local firms. The technical progress did not only take place in the MNEs' own industries, but also in other sectors, because the foreign affiliates forced domestic firms to modernize by imposing on them minimum standards of quality, delivery schedules, prices, etc., in their supplies of parts and raw materials (Katz, 1969: 154). The volume of vertical backward linkages generated is determined by two decisions concerning the sourcing of raw materials and intermediate products of the firm: 'import or procure locally', and 'make or buy'.

A number of studies have compared the dependence of foreign and local firms on imported raw materials in order to get an idea of the extent of linkages generated in the domestic economy, as the local content in production is an indicator of the strength of local linkages. Foreign affiliates can be expected to import a higher proportion of their raw materials and other inputs than local firms, because of their familiarity with foreign suppliers and the alleged inadequacies of local producers (see McAleese and McDonald, 1978), and sometimes to provide a market for the products of their associates elsewhere. Cohen (1975), in the case of South Korea, Taiwan and Singapore, and Reidel (1975), in the case of Taiwan, have found export-oriented foreign firms importing a greater proportion of their inputs than their local counterparts. Even foreign firms producing predominantly for domestic markets have been found to depend more on imports than their local counterparts in studies by Kelkar (1977) and Subrahmanian and Pillai (1979) for India; McAleese and McDonald (1978) for Ireland; Jo (1980) for South Korea; and Newfarmer and Marsh (1981) for the Brazilian electrical industry. Lall and Streeten (1977), however, in a study of six countries including India, did not find any significant difference between the import dependence of foreign and local firms. Kumar (1990a: chapter 4) also did not find a statistically significant difference between the import dependence of foreign and local firms across forty-three branches of Indian manufacturing. Siddharthan and Safarian (1994), in a study of 640 large Indian corporations for the period of 1987–90, found that imports of disembodied technology were accompanied by greater imports of embodied technology in the form of capital goods.

The 'make or buy' decision actually relates to the degree of vertical integration. The latter is inversely related to sub-contracting parts of the production run to unassociated vendors. In countries such as India, which have evolved a strict trade and exchange control regime that restricts the freedom of firms to import, sub-contracting may be an important aspect of a firm's decision-making concerning the sourcing of intermediates and raw materials. A number of market failures may tempt a firm to internalize the manufacture of intermediate inputs, such as the certainty of delivery schedules and quality standards (Williamson, 1975; Jansson, 1982). A certain monopoly rent may also be associated with vertical integration. On the other hand, firms can internalize a part of the scale economies in the manufacture of intermediates and can escape problems of industrial relations by sub-contracting their production to other firms. Cohen (1975) found that, among the export oriented enterprises in Taiwan, South Korea and Singapore, local firms had a greater degree of vertical integration. Newfarmer and Marsh (1981) and Willmore (1986) found a reverse pattern in the case of Brazil. Lall (1980c) did not find any significant difference between the extent of sub-contracting of a foreign subsidiary and a local company in India, both producing trucks. Kumar (1990a: chapter 4) found foreign-controlled firms to have a greater extent of vertical integration than their local counterparts in his study of forty-three Indian manufacturing industries, even after controlling for firm size, profitability and financial variables in the framework of multivariate analysis.

Training and employee mobility

Some studies have documented the spillovers from FDI to local economies in the form of on-the-job training imparted by MNE affiliates to their personnel and through the mobility of trained personnel. Gerschenberg (1987) examined the detailed career data for seventy-two top- and middle-level managers in forty-one manufacturing firms, and concluded that MNE affiliates offer more training to their managers than local private firms, although the mobility seemed to be lower for managers employed by MNEs than for those in private local firms. Chen (1983) reported significantly higher training expenditures on the part of MNE affiliates in Hong Kong over local firms in three of the four industries sampled.

POLICY IMPLICATIONS

The nature of the relationship between technology imports and local R&D has important implications for technology policy formulation aimed at building up local technological capability in the country. However, empirical evidence has been mixed, owing perhaps to the many interactions making the relationship rather complex. One factor, however, that turns out to be important in determining the nature of the relationship is the mode of technology imports. In the internal or FDI mode of technology imports, the technology supplier retains the controlling stake in the enterprise. The bulk of FDI worldwide is undertaken by multinational enterprises. The technology recipient enterprise becomes a link in the global chain of affiliates subject to centralized decision-making. The location of R&D, as of production and sourcing, is generally subject to centralized decision-making, owing to its strategic importance to global operations. Hence, the affiliate in a developing country undertakes local R&D only if it fits in with the global strategy of the enterprise. Although, over the years, MNEs have shown a tendency to decentralize their R&D activity geographically, it is still concentrated largely in industrialized countries.

On the other hand, in the case of technology imports under contractual modes, such as licensing unaccompanied by ownership of the technology supplier, it is possible for the importer selectively to delink and build up technological capability with further technological effort in trying to absorb, assimilate and adapt the knowledge once imported. A lesson to be learnt from the experiences of Japan and South Korea in building technological capability is about delinking technology imports and capital imports to retain the freedom of decision-making for performing local R&D. It is evident that both these East Asian countries imported a large volume of technology, but much of the technology has been imported under contractual modes, outright licensing or through capital goods imports. These technology imports were followed up by further technological effort locally to absorb it through the process of reverse engineering. Thus the first generation of manufacturing plants in these countries were built by foreign technology licensors. The second generation of plants were built locally with the knowledge absorbed through reverse engineering. The next generation of plants were not only built locally but had been suitably updated, and incorporated cost-saving improvements (see Westphal et al., 1979; Bagchi, 1987; Amsden, 1991; Kim, 1997, among others). This would not have been possible had Japan and South Korea imported technology under an FDI package.

This strategy of importing technology through contractual modes, however, can succeed only in countries having high absorptive capacity. In the absence of adequate skills for the absorption of knowledge and building upon it, this strategy will be of limited value. In fact it may result in repetitive imports of technology for updating, as the off-the-shelf purchase of technology does not allow possibilities for continuous updating. FDI may be a better option in such cases, as the supplier may feel more inclined regularly to update the technology because of his stake in the venture. Furthermore, the right kind of technology may not be available on a contractual basis in the absence of adequate local technological capability.

Finally, the nature of the technology imports policy itself may have some implications for the nature of the relationship between technology imports and local R&D. A too restrictive policy regime towards technology imports may create a situation of virtual monopoly for the existing firms, leaving hardly any compulsion for product improvements or cost savings and thus choking any technological dynamism on the part of the firm. On the other hand, a too liberal policy for technology imports may discourage local R&D because of its several monopolistic attractions over local technologies (Kumar, 1990c). A limited degree of protection to local technology is, therefore, desirable. A somewhat selective policy on technology imports may encourage local technological development by restricting imports. However, their effectiveness would depend upon the enforcement mechanisms and administration. Some authors have argued for protection in the form of a tax on technology imports (see Kumar, 1990c; Fikkert, 1993) which has the advantage of being more transparent and less discretionary and hence less bureaucratic in nature. Another complementary means of protection to local technological effort is through infrastructural and financial support and the subsidization of business enterprise R&D, as has been widespread in industrialized countries.

The evidence on knowledge spillovers from FDI in the host economy that could raise the productivity of local competing enterprises is rather mixed, suggesting that some countries have been able to harness the positive externalities of FDI more than others. Local enterprises that have some technological strength generally benefit from the 'competitive spur' provided by the entry of a foreign competitor, while technologically weak national firms tend to be affected adversely by foreign entry. Therefore, the nature of spillovers would depend upon the strength of local enterprises. It is for this reason that governments in developing countries tend to take a phased approach to the liberalization of their markets to MNEs, in order to provide weaker local enterprises enough time to develop some capabilities. FDI and technology imports could also have considerable spillovers of knowledge to the host economy through vertical inter-firm linkages and employee mobility. These spillovers have been found to have been facilitated by a somewhat softer regime of intellectual property protection. The host governments may also adopt complementary policies to enable these spillovers to take place through different channels, such as the development of vertical inter-firm linkages between enterprises and ensuring employee mobility from foreign-owned enterprises to local small and medium enterprises.

BIBLIOGRAPHY

Acs, Z.J. and D.B. Audretsch (1987) 'Innovation, market structure, and firm size', *The Review of Economics and Statistics*, 71: 567–74.

—— (1988) 'Innovation in large and small firms: An empirical analysis', *American Economic Review*, 78: 678–90.

Agarwal, J.P. (1985) *Pros and Cons of Third World Multinationals: A Case Study of India*, Kieler Studien 195, Tübingen: J.C.B. Mohr.

—— (1990) 'Determinants of FDI in Pacific-Rim Developing Countries', *Asian Economic Review*, 32(1): 83–100.

Agarwal, J.P., Andrea Gubitz and Peter Nunnenkamp (1991) *Foreign Direct Investment in Developing Countries: The Case of Germany*, Kieler Studien 238, Tübingen: J.C.B. Mohr.

Aharoni, Yair and Seev Hirsch (1993). 'Enhancing the Competitive Advantage of Developing Countries in Technology-Intensive Industries: A Conceptual Scheme and Policy Implications', Copenhagen: Copenhagen Business School, WP 1–93.

Ahiakpor, James C.W. (1986a) 'The Profits of Foreign Firms in a Less Developed Country: Ghana', *Journal of Development Economics*, 20: 321–35.

—— (1986b) 'The Capital Intensity of Foreign, Private Local and State Owned Firms in a Less Developed Country', *Journal of Development Economics*, 20: 145–62.

Aitken, Brian, Gordon H. Hanson and Ann E. Harrison (1994) 'Spillovers, Foreign Investment and Export Behaviour', NBER Working Paper 4967, Cambridge, MA: NBER.

Aitken, Brian and Ann Harrison (1993) 'Do Domestic Firms Benefit from Foreign Direct Investment? Evidence from Panel Data', Policy Research Working Paper 1248, Washington DC: The World Bank.

Alcorta, Ludovico (1995) 'The Impact of Industrial Automation on Industrial Organisation: Implications for Developing Countries' Competitiveness', Discussion Paper 9508, Maastricht, Netherlands: UNU/INTECH.

Amsden, Alice (1989) *Asia's Next Giant: South Korea and Late Industrialization*, New York: Oxford University Press.

Angelmar, R. (1985) 'Market structure and research intensity in high-technology-opportunity industries', *Journal of Industrial Economics*, 34: 69–79.

Arora, Ashish (1991) 'Indigenous Technological Efforts and Imports of Technology: Complements or Substitutes?', Carnegie Mellon University, mimeo.

Athukorala, Premchandra and S.K. Jayasuriya (1988) 'Parentage and Factor Proportions: A Comparative Study of Third World Multinationals in Sri Lankan Manufacturing', *Oxford Bulletin of Economics and Statistics*, 50(4): 409–23.

Athukorala, Premchandra, Sisira Jayasuriya and Edward Oczkowski (1995) 'Multinational Firms and Export Performance in Developing Countries: Some Analytical Issues and New Empirical Evidence', *Journal of Development Economics*, 46: 109–22.

Audretsch, D.B. and Hideki Yamawaki (1988) 'R&D rivalry, industrial policy and US–Japanese trade', *Review of Economics and Statistics*, 70: 438–47.

Bagchi, Amiya Kumar (1987) *Public Intervention and Industrial Restructuring in China, India and Republic of Korea*, New Delhi: ILO-ARTEP.

Bain, Joe S. (1956) *Barriers to New Competition: Their Character and Consequences in Manufacturing Industries*, Cambridge, MA: Harvard University Press.

Balasubramanyam, V.N. and M.A. Salisu (1991) 'Export Promotion, Import Substitution and Direct Foreign Investment in Less Developed Countries', in A. Koekkoek and L.B.M. Mennes (eds), *International Trade and Global Development*, Essays in Honour of Jagdish Bhagwati, London: Routledge; 191–210.

Baldwin, Robert E. (1979) 'Determinants of Trade and Foreign Investment: Further Evidence', *Review of Economics and Statistics*, 61, 40–8.

Basant, Rakesh and Brian Fikkert (1993) 'The effects of R&D, foreign technology purchase, and domestic and international spillovers on productivity in Indian firms', *The Review of Economics and Statistics*, 78: 187–99.

Bell, Martin, Don Scott-Kemmis and Wit Satyarakwit (1982) 'Limited earning in infant industry: A case study', in F. Stewart and J. James (eds), *The Economics of New Technology in Developing Countries*, London: Frances Pinter; 138–55.

Bergsten, C. Fred, Thomas Horst and Theodore Moran (1978) *American Multinationals and American Interests*, Washington DC: Brookings Institution.

Blomström, Magnus (1986) 'Multinational and Market Structure in Mexico', *World Development*, 14: 523–30.

—— (1989) *Foreign Investment and Spillovers: A Study of Technology Transfer to Mexico*, London: Routledge.

—— (1990) *Transnational Corporations and Manufacturing Exports from Developing Countries*, New York: United Nations Centre on Transnational Corporations.

Blomström, Magnus and Edward N. Wolff (1989) 'Multinational Corporations and Productivity Convergence in Mexico', NBER Working Paper 3141, Cambridge.

Blumenthal, Tuvia (1979) 'A Note on the Relationship between Domestic Research and Development and Imports of Technology', *Economic Development and Cultural Change*, 27: 303–6.

Bonturi, Marcos and Kiichiro Fukasaku (1993) *Intra-Firm Trade*, Trade Policy Issues No. 1, OECD, Paris.

Bosworth, Derek L. (1980) 'The Transfer of US Technology Abroad', *Research Policy*, 9: 378–88.

Bound, J., C. Cummins, Z. Griliches, B.H. Hall and A. Jaffe (1984) 'Who does R&D and who patents?', in Z. Griliches (ed.), *R&D patents, and productivity*, Chicago: Chicago University Press for NBER; 21–54.

Braga, Helson and Larry Willmore (1991) 'Technological Imports and Technological Effort: An Analysis of their Determinants in Brazilian Firms', *The Journal of Industrial Economics*, 39: 421–32.

Branch, B. (1974) 'Research and Development Activity and Profitability', *Journal of Political Economy*, 82: 999–1011.

Buckley, Peter J. and Marc Casson (1976) *The Future of the Multinational Enterprise*, London: Macmillan.

Buckley, Peter J. and Robert D. Pearce (1981) 'Market Servicing by Multinational Manufacturing Firms: Exporting Versus Foreign Production', *Managerial and Decision Economics*, 2: 229–46.

Cantwell, John (1989) *Technological Innovation and Multinational Corporations*, Oxford: Basil Blackwell.

Caves, Richard E. (1971) 'International Corporations: The Industrial Economics of Foreign Investment', *Economica*, 38: 1–27.

—— (1974a) 'Causes of Direct Investment: Foreign Firms' Shares in Canadian and United Kingdom Manufacturing Industries', *Review of Economics and Statistics*, 56: 279–93.

—— (1974b) *International Trade, International Investment, and Imperfect Markets*, Special Papers in International Economics No. 10, Princeton, NJ: International Finance Section, Department of Economics, Princeton University.

—— (1996) *Multinational Enterprise and Economic Analysis*, Second Edition, Cambridge: Cambridge University Press.

Caves, Richard E. and M.E. Porter (1977) 'From Entry Barriers to Mobility Barriers: Conjectural Decisions and Contrived Deterrence to New Competition', *Quarterly Journal of Economics*, 91: 241–61.

Caves, Richard E., Michael E. Porter and A. Michael Spence, with John T. Scott (1980) *Competition in the Open Economy: A Model Applied to Canada*, Cambridge, MA: Harvard University Press.

Chen, Chug, Lawrence Chang and Yimin Zhang (1995) 'The Role of Foreign Direct Investment in China's Post-1978 Economic Development', *World Development*, 23: 691–703.

Chen, Edward K.Y. (1983) *Multinational Corporations, Technology and Employment*, London: Macmillan.

Cohen, B. (1975) *Multinational Firms and Asian Exports*, New Haven, CT: Yale University Press.

Cohen, W.M. (1995) 'Empirical Studies of Innovative Activity', in Paul Stoneman (ed.), *Handbook of the Economics of Innovation and Technological Change*, Oxford: Blackwell; 182–264.

Cohen, W.M. and R.C. Levin (1989) 'Empirical Studies of Innovation and Market Structure', in R. Schmalensee and R.D. Willing (eds), *Handbook of Industrial Organisation*, Volume II, Amsterdam: North-Holland.

Cohen, W.M., R.C. Levin and David C. Mowery (1987) 'Firm-size and R&D Intensity: A Re-examination', *The Journal of Industrial Economics*, 35(4): 543–65.

Cohen, W.M. and D.A. Levinthal (1989) 'Innovation and Learning: The Two Faces of R&D', *The Economic Journal*, 99: 569–96.

Comanor, W.S. (1967) 'Market Structure Product Differentiation and Industrial Research', *Quarterly Journal of Economics*, 81: 639–57.

Connolly, R.A. and M. Hirschey (1984) 'R&D, Market Structure and Profits: A Value-based Approach', *Review of Economics and Statistics*, 66: 682–6.

Connor, J.M. (1977) *The Market Power of Multinationals, A Quantitative Analysis of U.S. Corporations in Brazil and Mexico*, New York: Praeger.

Connor, J.M. and W.F. Mueller (1977) *Market Power and Profitability of Multinational Corporations in Brazil and Mexico*, U.S. Senate, Washington, DC: G.P.O.

—— (1982) 'Market Structure and Performance of US Multinationals in Brazil and Mexico', *Journal of Development Studies*, 18: 329–53.

Contractor, Farok J. (1990) 'Do Government Policies Toward Foreign Investment Matter?', GSM Working Paper No. 90–15, Newark, NJ: Rutgers University.

Cooper, Charles (1980) 'Policy Interventions for Technological Innovations in Developing Countries', Staff Working Paper No. 441, Washington DC: The World Bank.

—— (1991) 'Are Innovation Studies on Industrialized Economies Relevant to Technology Policy in Developing Countries?', UNU/INTECH Working Paper No. 3, Maastricht: UNU/INTECH.

—— (ed.) (1994) *Technology and Innovation in the International Economy*, Aldershot and Tokyo: Edward Elgar and the UNU Press.

—— (1995) 'Technology, Manufactured Exports and Competitiveness', Discussion Paper 9511, Maastricht: UNU/INTECH.

Cotsomitis, John, Chris DeBresson and Andy Kwan (1991) 'A Re-examination of the Technology Gap Theory of Trade: Some Evidence from Time Series Data for O.E.C.D. Countries', *Weltwirtschaftliches Archiv*, 127: 792–9.

Dahlman, Carl J. (1984) 'Foreign Technology and Indigenous Technological Capability in Brazil', in Martin Fransman and Kenneth King (eds), *Technological Capability in the Third World*, London: Macmillan; 317–34.

Dahlman, Carl, Irfan ul Haque and Kenji Takeuchi (1995) 'The World Trading Environment', in Irfan ul Haque *et al.*, *Trade, Technologies, and International Competitiveness*, Washington DC: The World Bank; 155–78.

Dahlman, Carl J., Bruce Ross-Larson and Larry E. Westphal (1987) 'Managing Technological Development: Lessons from the Newly Industrializing Countries', *World Development*, 15(6): 759–75.

Dasgupta, Ajit and Natteri Siddharthan (1985) 'Industrial Distribution of Indian Exports and Joint Ventures Abroad', *Development and Change*, 16: 159–74.

Dasgupta, P. and J. Stiglitz (1980) 'Industrial Structure and the Nature of Innovative Activity', *Economic Journal*, 90: 266–93.

Davidson, W.H. and Donald G. McFetridge (1985) 'Key Characteristics in the Choice of International Technology Transfer', *Journal of International Business Studies*, 16 (Summer): 5–21.

Deiaco, E., E. Hornell and G. Vickery (eds) (1990) *Technology and Investment: Critical Issues for the 1990s*, London: Pinter.

Dembo, David, Clarence J. Dias and Ward Morehouse (1989) 'The Vital Nexus in Biotechnology: The Relationship Between Research and Production and Its Implications for Latin America', Council on International Public Affairs, New York (mimeo).

Dennekamp, Johannes G. (1995) 'Intangible Assets, Internalization and Foreign Direct Investment in Manufacturing', *Journal of International Business Studies*, 26(3): 493–504.

Deolalikar, Anil B. and Robert E. Evenson (1989) 'Technology Production and Technology Purchase in Indian Industry: An Econometric Analysis', *The Review of Economics and Statistics*, 71(4): 687–92.

Desai, Ashok V. (1980) 'The Origin and Direction of Industrial R&D in India', *Research Policy*, 9: 74–96.

—— (1983) 'Market Structure and Technology: Their Interdependence in Indian Industry', WEP Working Paper No. 117, Geneva: International Labour Office.

—— (1985) 'Indigenous and Foreign Determinants of Technical Change in Indian Industry', *Economic and Political Weekly*, 20 (Special Number): 2081–94.

—— (ed.) (1988) *Technology Absorption in Indian Industry*, New Delhi: Wiley Eastern.

Dijk, Pitou van and K.S. Chalapati Rao (1994) *India's Trade Policy and the Export Performance of Industry*, New Delhi: Sage.

Dosi, G. (1988) 'Sources, procedures and microeconomic effects of innovation', *Journal of Economic Literature*, 36: 1126–71.

Dosi, G., Keith Pavitt and Luc Soete (1990) *The Economics of Technical Change and International Trade*, London: Harvester Wheatsheaf.

Dunning, John H. (1979) 'Explaining Changing Patterns of International Production: In Defence of the Eclectic Theory', *Oxford Bulletin of Economics and Statistics*, 41: 269–96.

—— (1981) *International Production and Multinational Enterprise*, London: Allen and Unwin.

—— (1983) 'Market Power of the Firm and International Transfer of Technology', *International Journal of Industrial Organization*, 1: 333–51.

—— (1993) *Multinational Enterprises and the Global Economy*, Reading: Addison-Wesley.

Enos, J.L. (1991) *The Creation of Technological Capability in Developing Countries*, London: Pinter.

—— (1995) *In Pursuit of Science and Technology in Sub-Saharan Africa: The Impact of Structural Adjustment Programmes*, London and Tokyo: Routledge and UNU Press.

Ernst and Young (1993) *Biotech 94: Long Term Value – Short Term Hurdles*, San Francisco: Ernst and Young.

—— (1996) *European Biotech 96: Volatility and Value*, London: Ernst and Young International.

Esho, Hideki (1985) 'A Comparison of Foreign Direct Investment from India, South Korea and Taiwan by Size, Region and Industry', *Journal of International Economic Studies*, 1: 1–37.

Evans, P.B. (1977) 'Direct Investment and Industrial Concentration', *Journal of Development Studies*, 13: 272–80.

Evenson, Robert E. and Larry E. Westphal (1995) 'Technological Change and Technology Strategy', in J. Behrman and T.N. Srinivasan (eds), *Handbook of Development Economics*, Volume III: 2211–99.

Fairchild, Loretta G. (1977) 'Performance and Technology of United States and National Firms in Mexico', *Journal of Devlopment Studies*, 14: 14–34.

Fairchild, Loretta and Kim Sosin (1986) 'Evaluating Differences in Technological Activity between Transnational and Domestic Firms in Latin America', *Journal of Development Studies*, 22: 697–708.

Farber, S. (1981) 'Buyer Market Structure and R&D Effort: A Simultaneous Equations Model', *Review of Economics and Statistics*, 62: 336–45.

Ferrantino, Michael J. (1992) 'Technology Expenditures, Factor Intensity, and Efficiency in Indian Manufacturing', *The Review of Economics and Statistics*, 74: 689–700.

—— (1993) 'The Effect of Intellectual Property Rights on International Trade and Investment', *Weltwirtschaftliches Archiv*, 129: 300–31.

Fikkert, Brian (1993) 'An Open or Closed Technology Policy? The Effects of Technology Licensing, Foreign Direct Investment, and Technology Spillovers on R&D in Indian Industrial Sector Firms', unpublished PhD dissertation, New Haven, CT: Yale University.

Fransman, Martin (1986) *Technology and Economic Development*, London: Harvester Wheatsheaf.

Fransman, Martin and Kenneth King (eds) (1984) *Technological Capability in the Third World*, London: Macmillan.

Freeman, C. (1982) *The Economics of Industrial Innovation*, London: Frances Pinter.

—— (1995) 'The national system of innovation in historical perspective', *Cambridge Journal of Economics*, 19: 5–24.

Freeman, C. and J. Hagedoorn (1992) *Globalization of Technology*, FOP 322, Brussels: Commission of the European Communities.

Frischtak, Claudio R. (1989) 'The Protection of Intellectual Property Rights and Industrial Technology Development in Brazil', Industry and Energy Working Papers 13, Washington DC: The World Bank.

Galbraith, J.K. (1952) *American Capitalism: The Concept of Countervailing Power*, Boston: Houghton Mifflin.

Geroski, P.A. and R. Pomroy (1990) 'Innovation and the Evolution of Market Structure', *The Journal of Industrial Economics*, 38: 299–314.

Gershenberg, Irving (1987) 'The Training and Spread of Managerial Know-How, A Comparative Analysis of Multinational and Other Firms in Kenya', *World Development*, 15(7): 931–9.

Gershenberg, Irving and T.C.I. Ryan (1978) 'Does Parentage Matter? An Analysis of Transnational and Other Firms: An East African Case', *Journal of Developing Areas*, 13: 3–10.

Globerman, S. (1979) 'Foreign Direct Investment and "Spillover" Efficiency Benefits in Canadian Manufacturing Industries', *Canadian Journal of Economics*, 12: 42–56.

Goglio, A. (1993) 'Technology-Gap Theories of International Trade: A Survey', in UNCTAD, *Report of Ad Hoc Expert Group on Technology Policies in Open Developing Country Economies*, Geneva: UNCTAD/ITD/TEC/3.

Grabowski, H.G. (1968) 'The Determinants of Industrial Research and Development: A Study of the Chemical, Drug, and Petroleum Industries', *Journal of Political Economy*, 76: 292–306.

Grabowski, H.G. and D.C. Mueller (1978) 'Industrial Research and Development, Intangible Capital Stocks, and Firm Profit Rates', *Bell Journal of Economics*, 21: 209–35.

Griliches, Zvi (1995) 'R&D and Productivity: Econometric Results and Measurement Issues', in Paul Stoneman (ed.), *Handbook of the Economics of Innovation and Technological Change*, Oxford: Blackwell; 52–89.

Grossman, G.M. and Elhanan Helpman (1991) *Innovation and Growth in the Global Economy*, Cambridge, MA: The MIT Press.

Gruber, William H., Dileep Mehta and Raymond Vernon (1967) 'The R&D Factor in International Trade and International Investment of US Industries', *Journal of Political Economy*, 75: 20–37.

Gu, Shulin (1995) 'A Review of Reform Policy for the S&T System in China', Working Paper 17, Maastricht: UNU/INTECH.

Guisinger, Stephen E. *et al.* (1985) *Investment Incentives and Performance Requirements: Patterns of International Trade, Production and Investment*, New York: Praeger.

Gupta, V.K. (1983) 'A simultaneous determination of structure, conduct and performance in Canadian manufacturing', *Oxford Economic Papers*, 35: 281–301.

Haddad, Mona and Ann Harrison (1993) 'Are There Positive Spillovers from Direct Foreign Investment? Evidence from Panel Data for Morocco', *Journal of Development Economics*, 42: 51–74.

Hagedoorn, J. and J. Schakenraad (1991) 'The Internationalization of the Economy, Global Strategies and Strategic Global Alliances', EC Monitor-FAST Paper, Brussels.

Haksar, Vikram (1995) 'Externalities, Growth, and Technology Transfer: Applications to the Indian Manufacturing Sector, 1975–90', Washington, DC: International Monetary Fund, mimeo.

Hall, B.H. (1987) 'The Relationship between Firm Size and Firm Growth in the US Manufacturing Sector', *Journal of Industrial Economics*, 35: 583–606.

Haque, Irfan ul, Martin Bell, Carl Dahlman, Sanjaya Lall and Keith Pavitt (1995) *Trade, Technology and International Competitiveness*, EDI Development Studies, Washington, DC: The World Bank.

Hay, Donald A. and Derek J. Morris (1991) *Industrial Economics and Organization: Theory and Evidence*, Second Edition, Oxford: Oxford University Press.

Helleiner, G.K. (1973) 'Manufacturing Exports from Less Developed Countries and Multinational Firms', *Economic Journal*, 55: 21–47.

—— (1992) *Trade Policy, Industrialization, and Development: New Perspectives*, Oxford: Clarendon Press.

Helleiner, G.K. and R. Lavergne (1979) 'Intra-firm Trade and Industrial Exports to the United States', *Oxford Bulletin of Economics and Statistics*, 41: 297–311.

Helpman, Elhanan and Paul Krugman (1989) *Trade Policy and Market Structure*, Cambridge, MA: MIT Press.

Hennart, Jean-François (1982) *A Theory of Multinational Enterprise*, Ann Arbor: The University of Michigan Press.

Hirsch, Seev (1967) *Location of Industry and International Competitiveness*, Oxford: Clarendon Press.

—— (1970) 'Technological Factors in the Composition and Direction of Israel's Industrial Exports', in Raymond Vernon (ed.), *The Technology Factor in International Trade*, New York: NBER; 145–231.

—— (1976) 'An International Trade and Investment Theory of the Firm', *Oxford Economic Papers*, 28: 258–70.

Hufbauer G.C. (1966) *Synthetic Materials and the Theory of International Trade*, London: Gerald Duckworth.

Hughes, Kirsty (1986) *Export and Technology*, Cambridge: Cambridge University Press.

Husain, Ishrat and W. Jun Kwang (1992) 'Capital Flows to South Asian and ASEAN Countries', Washington DC: World Bank, International Economics Department, WPS 843, January.

Hymer, Stephen H. (1976) *The International Operations of National Firms: A Study of Direct Foreign Investment*, PhD dissertation (MIT 1960), Cambridge, MA: MIT Press.

Ito, Shoji (1986) 'Modifying Imported Technology by Local Engineers: Hypotheses and Case Study of India', *The Developing Economies*, 24(4): 334–48.

Jacobsson, Staffan (1993) 'The Length of the Infant Industry Period: Evidence from the Engineering Industry in South Korea', *World Development*, 21(3): 407–19.

Jaffe, A.B. (1986) 'Technological Opportunity and Spillovers of R&D', *American Economic Review*, 76: 984–1001.

Jansson, Hans (1982) *Interfirm Linkages in a Developing Economy: The Case of Swedish Firms in India*, Uppsala: Acta Universitatis Uppsaliensis, Studia Oeconomiae Negotiorum 14.

Jenkins, R. (1979) 'The Export Performance of Multinational Corporations in Mexican Industries', *Journal of Development Studies*, 15: 89–107.

Jo, Sung-Hwan (1980) 'Direct Private Investment', in Chong Kee Park (ed.), *Macroeconomic and Industrial Development in Korea*, Seoul: Korea Development Institute; 129–82.

Junne, Gerd, (1988) 'Incidence of Biotechnology Advances on Developing Countries', in Research and Information System for the Non-Aligned and Other Developing Countries, *Biotechnology Revolution and the Third World*, New Delhi: RIS; 193–206.

Justman, Moshe and Morris Teubal (1991) 'A Structuralist Perspective on the Role of Technology in Economic Growth and Development', *World Development*, 19(9): 1167–83.

Kamien, M.I. and N.L. Schwartz (1982) *Market Structure and Innovation*, Cambridge University Press, Cambridge.

Kaplinsky, Raphael (1984) 'Trade in Technology – Who, What, Where and When?', in Martin Fransman and Kenneth King (eds), *Technological Capability in the Third World*, London: Macmillan; 139–60.

—— (1991) 'TNCs in the Third World: Stability or Discontinuity?', *Millennium Journal of International Studies*, 20(2): 257–311.

—— (1995) *Easternization: Spread of Japanese Management Techniques to Developing Countries*, London and Tokyo: Frank Cass and UNU Press.

Katrak, Homi (1985) 'Imported Technology, Enterprise Size and R&D in a Newly Industrialising Country: The Indian Experience', *Oxford Bulletin of Economics and Statistics*, 47: 213–30.

—— (1990) 'Import of technology and the technological effort of Indian enterprises', *World Development*, 18: 371–81.

Katz, Jorge M. (1969) *Production Functions, Foreign Investment and Growth*, Amsterdam: North-Holland.

—— (1984) 'Technical Innovation, Industrial Organisation and Comparative Advantage of Latin American Metalworking Industries', in Martin Fransman and Kenneth King (eds), *Technological Capability in the Third World*, London: Macmillan; 113–36.

—— (1987) *Technology Creation in Latin American Manufacturing Industries*, New York: St. Martin Press.

Kelkar, Vijay (1977) 'Impact of Private Foreign Investments in India, 1964–74: An Economic Analysis', in Charan Wadhwa (ed.), *Some Problems of India's Economic Policy*, New Delhi: Tata McGraw Hill; 729–43.

Kim, Linsu (1988) 'Technological Transformation in Korea and its Implications for Other Developing Countries', *Development and South–South Cooperation*, 4(7): 19–29.

—— (1993) 'National System of Industrial Innovation: Dynamics of Capability Building in Korea', in Richard R. Nelson (ed.), *National Innovation Systems: A Comparative Analysis*, Oxford: Oxford University Press; 357–83.

—— (1997) *Imitation to Innovation: The Dynamics of Korea's Technological Learning*, Boston, MA: HBS Press.

Kindleberger, C.P. (1969) *American Business Abroad: Six Lectures on Direct Investment*, New Haven, CT: Yale University Press.

Kirim A.S. (1986) 'Transnational Corporations and Local Capital: Comparative Conduct and Performance in the Turkish Pharmaceutical Industry', *World Development*, 14: 503–22.

Kloppenburg, Jack Jr. and Daniel Lee Kleinman (1988) 'The Genetic Resources Controversy', in Research and Information System for the Non-Aligned and Other Developing Countries, *Biotechnology Revolution and the Third World*, New Delhi: RIS; 279–313.

Koechlin, Timothy (1992) 'The Determinants of the Location of USA Direct Foreign Investment', *International Review of Applied Economics*, 6(2): 203–16.

Kojima, Kiyoshi (1978) *Direct Foreign Investment*, London: Croom Helm.

Kokko, A. (1994) 'Technology, Market Characteristics and Spillovers', *Journal of Development Economics*, 43: 279–93.

Komen, John and Gabrielle Persley (1993) 'Agricultural Biotechnology in Developing Countries: a Cross Country Review', Research Report No. 2, Intermediary Biotechnlogy Service, ISNAR, The Hague.

Kondo, Edson Kenji (1994) 'Patent Laws and Foreign Direct Investment: An Empirical Investigation', PhD dissertation, Boston, MA: Harvard University.

Krugman, Paul (1979) 'A Model of Innovation, Technology Transfer and the World Distribution of Income', *Journal of Political Economy*, 87: 253–66.

Kudrle, Robert T. (1984) 'The Correlates of Foreign Direct Investment in Developing Countries: A Look at Recent Experience', in Roger Benjamin and Robert T. Kudrle (eds), *The Industrial Future of the Pacific Basin*, Boulder, CO: Westview Press; 211–34.

Kumar, Nagesh (1984) 'Social Cost-benefit Analysis of an Export-oriented Project with Foreign Collaboration in India', *Industry and Development*, 10, UNIDO: 9–46.

—— (1986) 'Foreign Direct Investments and Technology Transfers among Developing Countries', in V.R. Panchamukhi, K.M. Raipuria, Rajesh Mehta and Nagesh Kumar, *The Third World and the World Economic System*, New Delhi: Radiant Publishers; 139–65.

—— (1987a) 'Foreign Investment and Export Orientation: The Case of India', in Seiji Naya, V. Vichit-Vadakan and U. Kerdpibule (eds), *Direct Foreign Investment and Export Promotion: Policies and Experiences in Asia*, Kuala Lumpur and Honolulu: SEACEN Research and Training Center and East–West Resource Systems Institute; 357–82.

—— (1987b) 'Technology Imports and Local Research and Development in Indian Manufacturing', *The Developing Economies*, 25: 220–33.

—— (1987c) 'Intangible Assets, Internationalisation and Foreign Production: Direct Investments and Licensing in Indian Manufacturing', *Weltwirtschaftliches Archiv*, 123: 325–45.

—— (1987d) 'Biotechnology in India', *Development: Seeds of Change* (Special Issue on Biotechnology), 4: 51–6.

—— (1988) 'Biotechnology Revolution and Third World: An Overview', in Research and Information System for the Non-Aligned and Other Developing Countries, *Biotechnology Revolution and the Third World*, New Delhi: RIS; 1–30.

—— (1990a) *Multinational Enterprises in India: Industrial Distribution, Characteristics and Performance*, London and New York: Routledge.

—— (1990b) 'Mobility Barriers and Profitability of Multinational and Local Enterprises in Indian Manufacturing', *The Journal of Industrial Economics*, 38: 449–61.

—— (1990c) 'Cost of Imported and Local Technologies: Implications for Technology Policy', *Economic and Political Weekly*, 25 (January 13): 103–6.

—— (1990d) 'Internalisation of Technology Transfer by U.S. Multinationals: A Transactions Cost Perspective', Paper presented at the Annual Meeting of the Academy of International Business, Toronto, October.

—— (1991) 'Mode of Rivalry and Comparative Behaviour of Multinational and Local Enterprises: The Case of Indian Manufacturing', *Journal of Development Economics*, 35: 381–92.

—— (1992a) *Single European Market, Multinationals and Industrial Reorganisation: Implications for Developing Countries*, Occasional Paper No. 37, New Delhi: RIS.

—— (1992b) 'Role of Government Intervention in the Commercialisation of Biotechnology: A Case Study of Filariasis Test Kit in India', in S. Visalakshi and S. Mohan (eds), *ELISA as Diagnostic Tool: Prospects and Implications*, New Delhi: Wiley Eastern; 73–82.

—— (1993) 'Biotechnologies and Sustainable Development: Potential and Constraints', in Michael C. Howard (ed.), *Asia's Environmental Crisis*, Boulder, CO: Westview Press; 69–179.

—— (1994a) 'Determinants of Export-orientation of Foreign Production by U.S. Multinationals: An Inter-Country Analysis', *Journal of International Business Studies*, 25(1): 141–56.

—— (1994b) *Multinational Enterprises and Industrial Organization: The Case of India*, New Delhi, Thousand Oaks and London: Sage Publications.

—— (1994c) 'Regional Trading Blocs, Industrial Reorganizations and Foreign Direct Investments – The Case of Single European Market', *World Competition,* 18(2): 35–55.

—— (1995a) 'Industrialization, Liberalization and Two Way Flows of Foreign Direct Investments: The Case of India', *Economic and Political Weekly*, 30: 3228–37; also reprinted in J.H. Dunning and R. Narula (eds), *Foreign Direct Investment and Governments: Catalysts for Economic Restructuring*, London: Routledge, 1996; 348–79.

—— (1995b) *Foreign Direct Investment, Technology Transfer and Exports of Developing Countries: Trends and Policy Implications*, Vienna: UNIDO ID/WG.542/6 (Spec.); also UNU/INTECH Discussion Paper 9507.

—— (1995c) 'Changing Character of Foreign Direct Investment from Developing Countries: Case Studies from Asia', Discussion Paper 9516, Maastricht: UNU/INTECH.

—— (1996a) 'Multinational Enterprises, New Technologies and Export-Oriented Industrialisation in Developing Countries: Trends and Prospects', Discussion Paper 9602, Maastricht: UNU/INTECH.

—— (1996b) 'Intellectual Property Protection, Market Orientation and Location of Overseas R&D Activities by Multinational Enterprises', *World Development*, 24(4): 673–88.

—— (1996c) 'Foreign Direct Investments and Technology Transfers in Development: A Perspective on Recent Literature', Discussion Paper 9606, Maastricht: UNU/INTECH.

Kumar, Nagesh and Mohammed Saqib (1996) 'Firm Size, Opportunities for Adaptation, and In-house R&D Activity in Developing Countries: The Case of Indian Manufacturing', *Research Policy*, 25(5): 712–22.

Kumar, Nagesh and N.S. Siddhartan (1994) 'Technology, Firm Size and Export Behaviour in Developing Countries: The Case of Indian Enterprises', *Journal of Development Studies*, 31(2): 289–309.

Kumar, Nagesh and Sundeep Waslekar (1994) *Developing Countries in the International Division of Labour in Design Engineering and Construction Services: The Case of India*, Occasional Paper No. 45, New Delhi: RIS.

Lall, S. (1976) 'Financial and Profit Performance of MNCs in Developing Countries: Some Evidence from an Indian and Columbian Sample', *World Development*, 4: 713–24.

—— (1978a) 'Transnationals, Domestic Enterprises and Industrial Structure in Host LDCs', *Oxford Economic Papers*, 30: 217–48.

—— (1978b) 'The Pattern of Intra-firm Exports by US Multinationals', *Oxford Bulletin of Economics and Statistics*, 40: 209–22.

—— (1979) 'Multinationals and Market Structures in Open Developing Countries: The Case of Malaysia', *Weltwirtschaftliches Archiv*, 115: 325–48.

—— (1980a) 'Monopolistic Advantages and Foreign Involvement by US Manufacturing Industry', *Oxford Economic Papers*, 32: 102–22.

—— (1980b) 'Vertical Inter-firm-linkages in LDCs: An Empirical Study', *Oxford Bulletin of Economics and Statistics*, 42(3): 203–26.

—— (1983) 'Determinants of R&D in a LDC: The Indian Engineering Industry', *Economics Letters*, 13: 379–83.

—— (1984) 'India's Technological Capacity: Effects of Trade, Industrial Science and Technology Policies', in Martin Fransman and Kenneth King (eds), *Technological Capability in the Third World*, London: Macmillan; 225–44.

—— (1985) 'Multinationals and Technology Development in Host Countries', in Sanjaya Lall, *Multinationals, Technology and Exports*, London: Macmillan; 114–31.

—— (1986) 'Technological Development and Export Performance in LDCs: Leading Engineering and Chemical Firms in India', *Weltwirtschaftliches Archiv*, 122: 80–91.

—— (1987) *Learning to Industrialize: The Acquisition of Technological Capability by India*, London: Macmillan.

—— (1995) 'The Creation of Comparative Advantage: The Role of Industrial Policy', and 'The Creation of Comparative Advantage: Country Experiences', in Irfan ul Haque *et al.*, *Trade, Technology and International Competitiveness*, Washington DC: The World Bank; 103–54.

Lall, Sanjaya and R. Kumar (1981) 'Firm Level Export Performance in an Inward Looking Economy: The Indian Engineering Industry', *World Development*, 9: 453–63.

Lall, Sanjaya and Shariff Mohammed (1983a) 'Multinationals in Indian Big Business: Industrial Characteristics of Foreign Investments in a Heavily Regulated Economy', *Journal of Development Economics*, 13: 143–57.

—— (1983b) 'Foreign Ownership and Expert Performance in the Large Corporate Sector of India', *Journal of Development Studies*, 20: 56–67.

Lall, S. and N.S. Siddharthan (1982) 'The Monopolistic Advantages of Multinationals: Lessons from Foreign Investment in the US', *Economic Journal*, 92: 668–83.

Lall, Sanjaya and P. Streeten (1977) *Foreign Investments, Transnationals and Developing Countries*, London: Macmillan.

Lall, Sanjaya, *et al.* (1983) *The New Multinationals*, Chichester: John Wiley.

Langdon, Steven (1984) 'Indigenous Technological Capability in Africa: The Case of Textiles and Wood Products in Kenya', in Martin Fransman and Kenneth King (eds), *Technological Capability in the Third World*, London: Macmillan; 355–74.

Levin, R.C., W.M. Cohen and D.C. Mowery (1985) 'R&D Appropriability, Opportunity, and Market Structure: New Evidence on Some Schumpeterian Hypotheses', *American Economic Review* (Papers and Proceedings), 75: 20–4.

Levin, Richard C. and Peter C. Reiss (1991) 'Test of a Schumpeterian Model of R&D and Market Structure', in Griliches, Z. (ed.), *R&D, Patents and Productivity*, Chicago and London: The University of Chicago Press; 175–204.

Loree, David W. and Stephen E. Guisinger (1995) 'Policy and Non-Policy Determinants of U.S. Equity Foreign Direct Investment', *Journal of International Business Studies*, 26(2): 281–300.

Lucas, Robert E. (1988) 'On the Mechanics of Economic Development', *Journal of Monetary Economics*, 22: 3–42.

—— (1993) 'On the Determinants of Direct Foreign Investment: Evidence from East and Southeast Asia', *World Development*, 21(3): 391–406.

Lundvall, Bengt-Ake (ed.) (1992) *National Systems of Innovation: Towards a Theory of Innovation and Interactive Learning*, London: Pinter.

Mansfield, E. (1964) 'Industrial Research and Development Expenditures: Determinants, Prospects, and Relation of Size of Firm and Inventive Output', *Journal of Political Economy*, 72: 319–40.

—— (1968) *Industrial Research and Technological Innovation: An Econometric Analysis*, Norton, New York.

—— (1981) 'Composition of R&D Expenditures: Relationship to Size, Concentration, and Innovation Output', *Review of Economics and Statistics*, 62: 610–14.

—— (1986) 'Patents and Innovation: An Empirical Study', *Management Science*, 32: 173–81.

—— (1994) 'Intellectual Property Protection, Foreign Direct Investment, and Technology Transfer', Discussion Paper 19, International Finance Cooperation, The World Bank, Washington, D.C.

Mansfield, Edwin, A. Romeo and S. Wagner (1979) 'Foreign Trade and US Research and Development', *Review of Economics and Statistics*, 61: 49–57.

Markusen, James R. (1995) 'The Boundaries of Multinational Enterprises and the Theory of International Trade', *Journal of Economic Perspectives*, 9(2): 169–89.

Marris, R. (1964) *The Economic Theory of Managerial Capitalism*, London: Macmillan.

Mayer-Krahmer, Frieder (1990) 'The Determinants of Investment in R&D and the Role of Public Policies: An Evaluation', in E. Deiaco, E. Hornell and G. Vickery (eds), *Technology and Investment: Critical Issues for the 1990s*, London: Pinter; 167–84.

McAleese, D. and Donogh McDonald (1978) 'Employment Growth and the Development of Linkages in Foreign-Owned and Domestic Manufacturing Enterprises', *Oxford Bulletin of Economics and Statistics*, 40: 321–39.

Megna, Pamela and Dennis Mueller (1991) 'Profit Rates and Intangible Capital', *Review of Economics and Statistics*, 73: 632–42.

Metcalfe, J.S. (1995) 'Technology Systems and Technology Policy in an Evolutionary Framework', *Cambridge Journal of Economics*, 19: 25–46.

Mody, Ashoka and David Wheeler (1990) *Automation and World Competition: New Technologies, Industrial Location and Trade*, Basingstoke: Macmillan.

Moore, Michael O. (1993) 'Determinants of German Manufacturing Direct Investment: 1980–1988', *Weltwirtschaftliches Archiv*, 129(1): 120–38.

Morgenstern, R.D. and R. Mueller (1976) 'Multinational Versus Local Corporations in LCDs: An Econometric Analysis of Export Performance in Latin America', *Southern Economic Journal*, 88: 59–84.

Mowery, David C. and Nathan Rosenberg (1989) *Technology and the Pursuit of Economic Growth*, Cambridge: Cambridge University Press.

Nayyar, Deepak (1978) 'Transnational Corporations and Manufactured Exports from Poor Countries', *Economic Journal*, 88: 59–84.

Nelson, R.R. (1959) 'The Simple Economics of Basic Scientific Research', *Journal of Political Economy*, 67: 297–306.

—— (ed.) (1993) *National Innovation Systems: A Comparative Analysis*, Oxford: Oxford University Press.

Nelson, R.R. and Sidney G. Winter (1982) *An Evolutionary Theory of Economic Change*, Cambridge and London: Harvard University Press.

Newfarmer, R.S. and L.C. Marsh (1981) 'Foreign Ownership, Market Structure and Industrial Performance – Brazil's Electrical Industry', *Journal of Development Economics*, 8: 47–75.

Newfarmer, R.S. and W.F. Mueller (1975) *Multinational Corporations in Brazil and Mexico: Structural Sources of Economic and Non-Economic Power*, US Senate, Washington, DC: GPO.

Odagiri, H. (1983) 'R&D Expenditure, Royalty Payments and Sales Growth in Japanese Manufacturing Corporations', *Journal of Industrial Economics*, 32: 61–7.

OECD (1992) *Biotechnology, Agriculture and Food*, Paris: OECD.

Orr, Dale (1974) 'The Determinants of Entry: A Study of the Canadian Manufacturing Industries', *Review of Economics and Statistics*, 56: 58–66.

Owen, Robert F. (1982) 'Inter-Industry Determinants of Foreign Direct Investments: A Canadian Perspective', in Alan M. Rugman (ed.) *New Theories of the Multinational Enterprise*, London, Croom Helm; 238–53.

Pack, H. (1992) 'Technology Gaps between Developed and Developing Countries: Are There Dividends for Latecomers?', Paper prepared for the World Bank's Annual Conference on Development Economics, Washington, D.C., April 30 and May 1.

Pack, H. and Larrry E. Westphal (1986) 'Industrial Strategy and Technological Change: Theory versus Reality', *Journal of Development Economics*, 22: 87–128.

Page, Sheila (1991) 'Europe 1992: Views of Developing Countries', *The Economic Journal*, 101: 1553–66.

Panchamukhi, V.R. (1994) 'Recent Developments in Trade Theory and Practice', Presidential Address at the Platinum Jubilee Session of the Indian Economic Association, Bombay.

Panchamukhi, V.R. and Nagesh Kumar (1988) 'Impact on Commodity Exports', in Research and Information System for the Non-Aligned and Other Developing Countries, *Biotechnology Revolution and the Third World*, New Delhi: RIS; 207–24.

Pandit, B.L. and N.S. Siddharthan (1997) 'Technological Acquisition and Investment: Lessons from Recent Indian Experience', *Journal of Business Venturing* (forthcoming).

Pant, Manoj (1995) *Foreign Direct Investment in India: The Issues Involved*, New Delhi: Lancers.

Patel, Surendra J. (1995) *Technological Transformation*, Volume V: *The Historic Process*, Aldershot: Avebury and UNU Press.

Pavitt, K., M. Robson and J. Townsend (1987) 'The Size Distribution of Innovating Firms in the UK: 1945–1983', *Journal of Industrial Economics*, 35: 297–316.

Phillips, A. (1966) 'Patents, Potential Competition, and Technical Progress', *American Economic Review*, 56, 301–10.

Porter, Michael E. (1979) 'The Structure within Industries and Companies' Performance', *Review of Economics and Statistics*, 61: 214–27.

Posner, Michael V. (1961) 'International Trade and Technical Change', *Oxford Economic Papers*, 13: 11–37.

Radhu, Ghulam (1973) 'Transfer of Technological Know-how through MNCs in Pakistan', *Pakistan Development Review*, 12: 361–74.

Ramstetter, Eric D. (ed.) (1991) *Direct Foreign Investment in Asia's Developing Economies and Structural Change in the Asia-Pacific Region*, Boulder, CO: Westview Press.

Rana, Pradumna B. (1988) 'Recent Trends and Issues on Foreign Direct Investment in Asian and Pacific Developing Countries', Economic Staff Paper No. 41, Manila: Asian Development Bank.

Rao, K.S. Chalapati (1994) 'An Evaluation of Export Policies and the Export Performance of Large Private Companies', in Pitou van Dijk and K.S. Chalapati Rao, *India's Trade Policy and the Export Performance of Industry*, New Delhi: Sage.

Raut, Lakshmi (1995) 'R&D Spillover and Productivity Growth: Evidence from Indian Private Firms', *Journal of Development Economics*, 48: 1–23.

Ray, E.J. (1981) 'Tariff and non-tariff barriers to trade in the US and abroad', *Review of Economics and Statistics*, 63: 161–8.

Reza, Sadrel, A.H.M.M. Alam and M. Ali Rashid (1986) 'The Balance of Payments Effect of Private Foreign Investment: A Case Study of Bangladesh', *Bangladesh Development Studies*, 14(3): 55–66.

Riedel, J. (1975) 'The Nature and Determinants of Export-oriented Direct Foreign Investment in a Developing Country: A Case Study of Taiwan', *Weltwirtschaftliches Archiv*, 111: 505–28.

RIS (1988) *Biotechnology Revolution and the Third World*, New Delhi: Research and Information System for the Non-Aligned and Other Developing Countries.

Romer, Paul M. (1986) 'Increasing Returns and Long-Run Growth', *Journal of Political Economy*, 94: 1002–37.

—— (1994) 'The Origins of Endogenous Growth', *Journal of Economic Perspectives*, 8(1): 3–22.

Roobeek, Annemieke (1990) *Beyond the Technology Race: An Analysis of Technology Policy in Seven Industrial Countries*, Amsterdam: Elsevier.

Root, Franklin and Ahmed Ahmed (1979) 'Empirical Determinants of Manufacturing Direct Foreign Investment in Developing Countries', *Economic Development and Cultural Change*, 27(4): 751–61.

Rothwell, R.C., A. Horsley Freeman, V.T.P. Jervis, A.B. Robertson and J. Townsend, (1974) 'SAPPHO Updated: Project SAPPHO phase II', *Research Policy*, 3: 258–91.

Rugman, Alan M. (1981) *Inside the Multinationals: The Economics of Internal Markets*, London: Croom Helm.

Saunders, Ronald S. (1982) 'The Determinants of Inter-industry Variation of Foreign Ownership in Canadian Manufacturing', *Canadian Journal of Economics*, 25: 77–84.

Scherer, F.M. (1965) 'Firm size, market structure, opportunity, and the output of patented inventions', *American Economic Review*, 55: 1097–125.

Scherer, F.M. (1967) 'Market structure and the employment of scientists and engineers', *American Economic Review*, 57: 524–31.

—— (1970) *Industrial Market Structure and Economic Performance*, Chicago: Rand McNally.

—— (1991) 'Changing perspectives on the firm size problem', in Z.J. Acs and D.B. Audretsch (eds), *Innovation and Technological Change: An International Comparison*, New York, Harvester Wheatsheaf; 24–38.

Scherer, F.M. and Richard S. Belous (1994) *Unfinished Tasks: The New International Trade Theory and the Post-Uruguay Round Challenges*, London and Washington: British–North American Committee.

Scherer, F.M. and S. Weisburst (1995) 'Economic Effects of Strengthening Pharmaceutical Patent Protection in Italy', *International Review of Industrial Property and Copyright Law*, 26(6): 1020–4.

Schmalensee, R. (1989) 'Inter-industry Studies of Structure and Performance', in R. Schmalensee and R.D. Willing (eds), *Hand Book of Industrial Organisation*, Volume II, Amsterdam: North-Holland; 951–1010.

Schmookler, J. (1962) 'Economic Sources of Inventive Activity', *Journal of Economic History*, 22: 1–10.

Schneider, Friedrich and Bruno S. Frey (1985) 'Economic and Political Determinants of Foreign Direct Investment', *World Development*, 13: 161–75.

Schumpeter, J.A. (1942) *Capitalism, Socialism, and Democracy*, New York: Harper.

Shrieves, R.E. (1978) 'Market Structure and Innovation: A New Perspective', *Journal of Industrial Economics*, 26: 329–47.

Siddharthan, N.S. (1984) 'Industrial Structure, Non-price Competition and Industrial Development', *Economic and Political Weekly*, 19 (Annual Number): 1307–10.

—— (1988) 'In-house R&D, Imported Technology and Firm Size: Lessons from Indian Experience', *Developing Economies*, 26: 212–21.

—— (1992) 'Transaction Costs, Technology Transfer, and In-house R&D: A Study of the Indian Private Corporate Sector', *Journal of Economic Behaviour and Organization*, 18: 265–71.

—— (1997) 'Differential Behaviour of the Japanese Affiliates in the Indian automobile sector', *Japan and the World Economy*, forthcoming.

Siddharthan, N.S. and R.N. Agarwal (1992) 'Determinants of R&D Decisions: A Cross Section Study of Indian Private Corporate Firms', *Economics of Innovation and New Technology*, 2: 103–10.

Siddharthan, N.S. and A. Dasgupta (1983) 'Entry Barriers, Exports and Inter-industry Differences in Profitability', *Developing Economies*, 21: 14–23.

Siddharthan, N.S. and K.L. Krishna (1994) 'Determinants of Technology Imports: Evidence for Indian Firms', Working Paper E/161/94, Delhi: Institute of Economic Growth.

Siddharthan, N.S. and Nagesh Kumar (1990) 'The Determinants of Inter-industry Variation in the Proportion of Intra-Firm Trade: The Behaviour of U.S. Multinationals', *Weltwirtschaftliches Archiv*, 126: 581–91.

Siddharthan, N.S. and S. Lall (1982) 'The Recent Growth of the Largest US Multinationals', *Oxford Bulletin of Economics and Statistics*, 44: 1–13.

Siddharthan, N.S. and B.L. Pandit (1992) 'Deregulations, Entry and Industrial Performance: The Impact of Recent Indian Policy Changes', *Indian Economic Review*, Special Issue in Honour of Professor S. Chakraverty: 277–384.

Siddharthan, N.S. and A.E. Safarian (1994) 'Technology Transfer and Import of Capital Goods: Recent Indian Experience', Institute of Economic Growth and Conference Board of Canada, mimeo.

Siddharthan, N.S., B.L. Pandit and R.N. Agarwal (1994) 'Growth and Profit Behaviour of Large Indian Firms', *Developing Economies*, 32: 188–209.

Sleuwaegen, Leo and Hideki Yamawaki (1991) 'Foreign Direct Investment and Intra-Firm Trade: Evidence from Japan', in Ad Koekkoek and L.B.M. Mennes (eds), *International Trade and Global Development (Essays in Honour of Jagdish Bhagwati)*, London: Routledge; 143–61.

Soete, Luc (1981) 'A General Test of Technological Gap Theory', *Weltwirtschaftliches Archiv*, 117: 638–59.

—— (1987) 'The Impact of Technological Innovation on International Trade Patterns: The Evidence Reconsidered', *Research Policy*, 16: 101–30.

Stewart, Frances (1984) 'Facilitating Indigenous Change in Third World Countries', in Martin Fransman and Kenneth King (eds), *Technological Capability in the Third World*, London: Macmillan; 81–94.

Subrahmanian, K.K. (1972) *Import of Capital and Technology*, New Delhi: Peoples Publishing House.

—— (1991) 'Technological Capability under Economic Liberalism: Experience of Indian Industry in Eighties', *Economic and Political Weekly*, 26 (August 31): M87–9.

Subrahmanian, K.K. and Mohanan P. Pillai (1979) *Multinationals and Indian Exports*, New Delhi: Allied.

Sveikauskas, Leo (1983) 'Science and Technology in United States Foreign Trade', *Economic Journal*, 93: 542–54.

Swedenborg, B. (1979) *The Multinational Operations of Swedish Firms*, Stockholm: IUI.

Tambunlertchai, Somsak and Eric D. Ramstetter (1991) 'Foreign Firms in Promoted Industries and Structural Change in Thailand', in Eric D. Ramstetter (ed.), *Direct Foreign Investment in Asia's Developing Economies and Structural Change in the Asia-Pacific Region*, Boulder, CO: Westview Press; 65–102.

Teece, David (1981) 'The Market for Know-how and Efficient International Transfer of Technology', *Annals of American Academy of Political and Social Science*, 458: 81–96.

—— (1983) 'Technological and Organisational Factors in the Theory of the Multinational Enterprise', in Mark C. Casson (ed.) *The Growth of International Business*, London: Macmillan; 51–62.

—— (1986) 'Profiting from Technological Innovation: Implications for Integration, Collaboration, Licensing and Public Policy', *Research Policy*, 15: 286–305.

Teubal, Morris, Dominique Foray, Moshe Justman and Zuscovitch Ehud (eds) (1996) *Technological Infrastructure Policy: An International Perspective*, Dordrecht, Boston and London: Kluwer.

Thomas, Sandra M. (1993) 'Global Perspective 2010: The Case of Biotechnology', a report for the FAST Programme, Commission of the European Communities, FOP 330, Brussels.

Tsai, Pan-Long (1991) 'Determinants of Foreign Direct Investment in Taiwan: An Alternative Approach with Time Series Data', *World Development*, 19(2/3): 275–85.

Tuldar, Rob van and Gerd Junne (1988) *European Multinationals in Core Technologies*, London: Wiley.

UNCTAD (1993) *Explaining and Forecasting Regional Flows of Foreign Direct Investment*, New York: United Nations.

—— (1995) *World Investment Report 1995*, Geneva: United Nations Conference on Trade and Development.

UNCTC (1992) *The Determinants of Foreign Direct Investment: A Survey of the Evidence*, New York: United Nations.

UNIDO (1991) *Biotechnology Policies and Programmes in Developing Countries: Survey and Analysis*, Technology Trends Series No. 14, IPCT.135, Vienna: UNIDO.

United Nations (1992) *Biotechnology and Development: Expanding the Capacity to Produce Food*, Advanced Technology Assessment System Issue No. 9, Winter, New York: United Nations.

van Hulst, Noe, Ronald Mulder and Luc Soete (1991) 'Exports and Technology in Manufacturing Industry', *Weltwirtschaftliches Archiv*, 127: 246–63.

Vernon, Raymond (1966) 'International Investment and International Trade in the Product Cycle', *Quarterly Journal of Economics*, 80: 190–207.

—— (1990) 'Trade and Technology in the Developing Countries', in Robert Evenson and Gustav Ranis (eds), *Science and Technology: Lessons for Development Policy*, Boulder, CO and San Francisco: Westview Press; 255–70.

Wade, Robert (1990) *Governing the Market: Economic Theory and the Role of Government in East Asian Industrialization*, Princeton, NJ: Princeton University Press.

Walsh, V. *et al.* (1991) 'The Globalization of the Technology and the Economy: Implications and Consequences for the Scientific and Technology Policy of the EC', a report for the FAST Programme, FOP 284, Brussels: Commission of the European Communities.

Wangwe, Samuel (1992) 'New Trade Theories and Developing Countries: Policy and Technological Implications', UNU/INTECH Working Paper No. 7, Maastricht: UNU/INTECH.

—— (1995) *Exporting Africa: Technology, Trade and Industrialization in Sub-Saharan Africa*, London and New York: Routledge and UNU Press.

Weiss, Charles Jr (1992) 'The Value-Added Ladder in Agricultural Biotechnology', in United Nations *Biotechnology and Development: Expanding the Capacity to Produce Food*, New York: The United Nations; 235–6.

Wells, L.T. (1983) *Third World Multinationals: The Rise of Foreign Investment from Developing Countries*, Cambridge, MA: MIT Press.

—— (1993) 'Mobile Exporters: New Foreign Investors in East Asia', in K.A. Froot (ed.), *Foreign Direct Investment*, Chicago: Chicago University Press and NBER; 173–91.

Westphal, Larry E., Y.W. Rhee and Garry Pursell (1979) 'Foreign Influences on Korean Industrial Development', *Oxford Bulletin of Economics and Statistics*, 41: 359–88.

Wheeler, David and Ashoka Mody (1992) 'International Investment, Location Decisions: The Case of U.S. Firms', *Journal of International Economics*, 33: 57–76.

Williamson, Oliver H. (1975) *Markets and Hierarchies: Analysis and Antitrust Implications: A Study in the Economics of Internal Organisation*, New York: Free Press.

—— (1981) 'The Modern Corporation, Origins, Evolution, Attributes', *Journal of Economic Literature*, 19; 499–518.

Willmore, L.N. (1976) 'Direct Foreign Investment in Central American Manufacturing', *World Development*, 4: 499–518.

—— (1986) 'The Comparative Performance of Foreign and Domestic Firms in Brazil', *World Development*, 14: 489–502.

—— (1989) 'Determinants of Industrial Structure: A Brazilian Case Study', *World Development*, 17: 1601–17.

—— (1992) 'Transnationals and Foreign Trade: Evidence from Brazil', *The Journal of Development Studies*, 28: 314–35.

World Bank (1995) *Global Economic Prospects and the Developing Countries 1995*, Washington DC: The World Bank.

INDEX